BELOW THE ZONE

Also by General Merrill A. McPeak

Hangar Flying

Below the Zone

GENERAL MERRILL A. MCPEAK
Former Chief of Staff, US Air Force

Lost Wingman Press
Lake Oswego, Oregon

LOST WINGMAN PRESS

123 Furnace Street, Lake Oswego, OR 97034

www.LostWingmanPress.com

18 17 16 15 14 13   1 2 3 4 5

Editor: Holly Franko

Illustrations: Keith Buckley

Cover and book design: Jennifer Omner

Set in Myriad Pro and Century Schoolbook

PUBLISHER'S CATALOGING-IN-PUBLICATION DATA

McPeak, Merrill A., 1936–
     Below the zone / General Merrill A. McPeak.
          p. cm.
     Includes index.
     ISBN: 978-0-9833160-4-6 (hardcover)
     ISBN: 978-0-9833160-5-3 (pbk.)
     ISBN: 978-0-9833160-6-0 (e-book)
     ISBN: 978-0-9833160-7-7 (leatherbound)
     1. McPeak, Merrill A., 1936– 2. United States. Air Force—
Generals—Biography. 3. Fighter pilots—United States—
Biography. 4. Cold War—History.   I. Title.
UG626 . M4352 A3 2013
358.4`0092—dc23

                                        2013901036

For Mark

Contents

Preface

My career took the sonata form. A dozen or so years of cockpit duty supplied themes for an *allegro* first movement, published as *Hangar Flying*. The turbulent 1960s furnished a stage, the Cold War durable scenery, but the themes themselves echoed an oral tradition begun when pioneer airmen huddled around the stove on those bad-weather days and told stories about what they had done in the sky. Often these stories had a plot, some character development, a sense of time and place—all the properties of good fiction. But of course they were not in any way imaginary. The facts would have been polished, but the stories themselves were always true— true to the circumstances, to the individual, to history.

The tempo slowed in a middle movement, the 20-year *andante* described here. Certainly, the Soviet threat imposed a constant, high state of readiness, but military professionals will recognize the motif: peacetime, in-garrison administration. For me, it was a time spent climbing the rungs of a large, complicated organization, a time of both rapid and slow promotion, of elation and disappointment, of good jobs and jobs I knew must be horrible, though as it turned out I never had a bad job.

The opportunities and challenges took me to a variety of settings, making *Below the Zone* a sort of travelogue. But I intend something more: a modest contribution to the glut of how-to books on leadership and management currently warping library shelves. As this volume opens, I'd already had one or two short-term staff jobs, but the primary focus had been on membership in small units. In formations of squadron size or smaller, everybody knows everybody else, and the leadership qualities that count are, first, you must be competent—able to perform the task at hand yourself, and do it pretty well—and second, you must be trusted by teammates. These would not seem to be lofty goals: to be skilled at a job and deserving of trust. But in the military profession, these qualities have weighty implications: competence means the ability to prevail in a fight to the death against determined opposition. And the trust must come from people who understand that their lives, too, are at stake. Given these conditions, there is no such thing as being too competent, or too trustworthy. In small units, both qualities are necessary; together they are enough.

Now, in the 1970s and '80s, I entered the world of medium- and large-sized organizations, a much more cluttered landscape, a zone of increasing ambiguity—the world of politics, broadly defined. To be sure, competence and trustworthiness continued to matter, but they would no longer suffice. Worse, these noble qualities often were (or seemed to be) in tension with each other. In these pages we will hear much less the incorruptible voice of the fighter pilot. Instead, a seasoned executive speaks of trade-offs, of the large and small compromises made getting to the top of any sizable organization, and then keeping it from jumping the tracks.

Of course, it was during this 20-year period that we won the Cold War, though we should be precise about what actually happened: the Soviets lost it.

A *presto* finale is still to come and must be written in yet another voice, that of a service chief, the uniformed head of one of our country's armed services.

Of all the Air Force's faults, the greatest has always been the fact that it has made its work seem too easy.
                                        —Gen. Henry H. "Hap" Arnold

Chapter 1

Middle East Desk

The active-duty promotion system . . . must provide reasonable opportunity for promotion, including accelerated promotion from below the zone for officers of exceptional potential.

—The Air Force Officer's Guide

It was January 1970, and we headed for the Armed Forces Staff College at Norfolk, Virginia, where I was to be a student in the 47th class. This was a grand assignment for a couple of reasons. First, AFSC was a joint school, attended by younger field-grade officers from all services and midlevel civilians from various government agencies. Some prestige was attached to being selected for this joint course, as opposed to the staff colleges run by each of the services. In addition, the school took six months instead of a year and did not feature an "optional" program to stay after hours and get a graduate degree. In short, it was the perfect way to decompress after a tour in Vietnam. The college supplied on-base quarters, a townhouse-style three-bedroom in which I started getting reacquainted with Ellie and the boys.

We were organized in seminars of about a dozen students. I made a friend of Wolf Gross, an Army officer and foreign area specialist, deeply knowledgeable about the Indian subcontinent. The Army educated its foreign area specialists about geographic regions and gave them assignments there. They learned the language and immersed themselves in the culture. Between wars, the Army can do this sort of thing, producing officers like China expert "Vinegar" Joe Stilwell who come in handy when there's a dustup in the part of the world they understand. By contrast, Navy and especially Air Force officers must keep technical skills sharp, leaving little time for this sort of career broadening.

One seminar mate, Marine Corps major "Ski" Modrzejewski, had been awarded the Congressional Medal of Honor. I became friends with another Marine, Chuck Pitman, a warrior type with a colorful record who would later attain three-star rank as head of Marine Corps Aviation.

The curriculum was built around guest lectures, mostly on leadership and management, delivered by eminent authorities in a large auditorium. We broke up into seminars for further course work, with a variety of assignments aimed at sharpening writing and briefing skills. As a graduation exercise, each seminar produced the campaign plan for an imagined joint operation, in those years the invasion of Albania. Of course, we needed to drop paratroops and land soldiers who would link up. The Air Force would provide transport, reconnaissance, and air cover; the Navy, maritime superiority and supply. The requirement for the Marines to make an amphibious landing was obvious to all intelligent observers. Moreover, we found a useful role for the Coast Guard, as they too had students in attendance. Not much originality here, but something for everyone. Having been stationed in the UK, I recognized the format: work to rule.

There was a program of extracurricular activities. The seminars organized teams and competed in a variety of sports, leading to the predictable result: lots of people banged up. A school gala demanded amateur entertainment. Four of us formed a country-and-western band, Old What's His Name and the Unknowns.

❧

At the end of April, President Nixon decided to invade Cambodia and roll up VC sanctuaries. The bombing we'd been doing there for some time had become a source of increasing agitation, and now massive demonstrations boiled up all across the country. In May, at Kent State University, Ohio National Guardsmen fired into a crowd, killing four students and wounding nine more. In a nifty move, Nixon dismissed Lt. Gen. Lewis Hershey as head of Selective Service, then promoted him to four-star rank.

❧

Toward the end of my stay at Armed Forces Staff College, we learned that one of the students, Army lieutenant colonel Bernie Loeffke, had been selected to become a White House Fellow. Loeffke had an unusual background. Born in Colombia to German parents, he grew up trilingual in English, Spanish, and German. He later added Russian and Chinese when he became the first officer to hold, in succession, posts as defense attaché in Moscow and Beijing.

I'd never heard of the White House Fellow program, but they made such a big deal of it I knew it must be something special. The Army had its act together on things like foreign area specialists and White House fellowships. But then, in peacetime, the Army needed to keep busy. We had the flying schedule.

❧

Staff College completed, I was assigned to the Pentagon in the summer of 1970. Ellie and I bought a house in the suburbs of Alexandria, Virginia, paying $40,500 for a four-bedroom split-level worth maybe $25,000. The move was one of the bad ones. Staff College students all graduated the same day and all wanted to vacate quarters immediately. This overloaded local moving companies, which booked the business anyway, hiring temporary help off park benches. Our household goods got rough treatment, many things lost entirely, a lot more delivered broken or in bad shape. We ended up renting furniture so we could get moved into the new house.

Our pet cat, Clarence, caused further commotion. We had boarded him in California because the Staff College didn't allow pets in base quarters. Following graduation, we'd arranged to have him flown to Washington, but as a baggage handler was loading his packing crate into the cargo bay he somehow got loose and jumped up into the aircraft's wheel well. The passengers were unloaded, the flight delayed, then canceled, as Clarence refused to cooperate. On a slow news day, wire services picked up the story, and a picture of Clarence appeared in newspapers across the country. Eventually, our celebrity cat was rescued and sent on to us.

The Fourth of July fell on a Saturday, and we decided to adjourn the fun of moving in and take the kids downtown. When we got there, antiwar protesters had taken over the Mall. It turned ugly, and I hustled the family back to the car.

Some would say this was my welcome home. In the years since, well-intentioned civilian friends have grumbled about the reception given those coming back from Vietnam. I don't believe professionals were ever much bothered. I certainly didn't need a hometown parade for doing my job.

But the experience removed any doubt that the country would be a while recovering its poise. Harvard, for instance, announced the end of campus ROTC programs.

Two hundred and seventy-eight West Pointers died in Vietnam, an honorable showing. Annapolis made a worthy contribution: 130 lost. This was the first hot war for the Air Force Academy, which had been producing graduates for only about a decade up to the high water mark of our involvement in Southeast Asia. Its graduates would eventually account for a staggering 5½ percent of total Air Force losses—141 of 2,584 airmen killed in action. Harvard College lost 19, matching Norwich University. Of course, such a comparison ignores Harvard's considerable contribution away from the battlefield, in Washington, where so many of its graduates helped shape policy.

In the Pentagon, I was assigned as a staff officer in the Directorate of Plans, part of the Office of the Deputy Chief of Staff (DCS), Plans and Operations. Several layers above me, the DCS Ops was Lt. Gen. Russ Dougherty, a lawyer who had long ago made the transition to operations. His brilliance made him a standout officer, but he was unlucky in the sense that staff service during three wars kept him from logging any serious combat time. By contrast, the chief himself was "Three Finger Jack" Ryan, so named because of an injury received when flak blew his hand off the controls of a B-24 during one of the Ploesti raids. Ryan stepped on the escalator I was riding up to work one morning and asked about my duties. I told him I worked for him and he offered condolences, saying he had managed to delay his first Air Staff tour until he was a three-star. Set and match to him.

My job title was air operations staff officer, but in the shorthand used by the Air Staff, I was an action officer, or AO, meaning that, with respect to some particular matter, I was to have responsibility for specific actions or positions to be taken by the Air Force. One of our major preoccupations was preparing the chief of staff for his various get-togethers, including most commonly the regularly scheduled meetings of the joint chiefs, but also for other appointments he might have—in his own office, with the secretary of defense, at the White House, or elsewhere, including his frequent trips out of the country. Often, an action officer got to brief the chief in person. Using a standard, bullet-style format, the AO also prepared papers the chief could use during the back and forth of actual meetings.

I liked the action officer system. When it worked as it should, the AO was given outline guidance and the authority to get the job done with as little interference as possible. Of course, any AO had layers of supervision between himself and the chief, but he also had ownership of the issue and was expected to break down doors, sleep at his desk, do whatever it took to work it. Not fix it—few problems are ever solved in Washington—but *work* it. Of course, briefing skills were very important, especially the ability to abandon prepared materials and make an impromptu pitch to the chief during his 20-second elevator ride on the way to the meeting. The most highly prized skill was being able to summarize an issue concisely and clearly in writing, since the chief often had no time for any kind of briefing, including one in the elevator. Thus, being an action officer was a make-or-break opportunity. If the issue you were working landed on the front page and if you had your act together, you could spend a lot of time talking to the boss. On the other hand, any incompetence or lack of preparation would be exposed without mercy.

The Plans part of DCS Plans and Operations was organized into a policy division that handled crosscutting issues like arms control, terrorism, or peacekeeping, and a regional division that covered various geographies. Initially, I was detailed to the Southeast Asia Branch, on the small team responsible for Laos, giving me a live problem to work. In the usual new-guy fashion, I began by following others around the halls of the Pentagon. I had not yet worked a single paper of my own when my supervisor came by to say I'd been volunteered to take up temporary residence across the hall in the Near East, Africa, and South Asia (NEAFSA) Branch.

Hostilities had been common along all of Israel's frontiers since the cease-fire that ended the Six-Day War in June 1967, but the so-called War of Attrition officially began in the spring of 1969, when Egypt escalated attacks on Israeli positions near the Suez Canal. Without much artillery forward, Israeli soldiers dug in, leaving it to their airmen—the Israeli Defense Force/Air Force, or IDF/AF— to respond. Air fighting along the canal became intense, taking on a Wild West aspect. ("Texas" was the name Israeli fighter pilots gave to the air arena in the western Sinai.) Given the geographic and demographic disparities between Israel and Egypt, the Israelis clearly would not be content to trade casualties indefinitely. With tensions rising, Secretary of State William Rogers proposed a new peace plan, based largely on UN Security Council Resolution 242, which called for Israel to withdraw inside boundaries existing before the Six-Day War. In November 1969, Israel rejected the proposal.

Until 1967, the IDF/AF relied on French aircraft of all types, but France embargoed arms sales to the whole region after the Six-Day War, a move that had practical consequence only for Israel. We'd stepped in to provide the F-4, which now entered the fray. In January 1970, the IDF/AF used the F-4's increased range to hit industrial targets around Cairo. In response, Egypt's President Nasser traveled to Moscow seeking more assistance. After some wavering, the Russians agreed to help, installing additional and more advanced surface-to-air missiles (SAMs) along the canal and in the Egyptian interior, and bringing in Russian pilots and SAM operators as "advisers." In turn, the IDF/AF targeted the improved Egyptian air defenses, a dangerous development since it virtually guaranteed personal combat between Israeli and Russian airmen. Secretary Rogers, trying to get the Israelis to back off, held out as inducement a package of improved air weaponry, including some of the electronic-warfare equipment and air-delivered munitions we'd developed for use against SAM-defended targets in Southeast Asia.

The air fighting reached a climax on 30 July 1970. In a good-sized dogfight in Egyptian airspace, the Israelis shot down five Egyptian MiG-21s flown by Russian pilots, losing no planes of their own.[1] Uneasy about the possibility of Russian retaliation and

---

1 As "advisers," the Russians had shown an arrogance that did not sit well with Egyptians. A joke about Russian military doctrine circulated through Egyptian ranks: Beating Israel was no problem. Just follow the Russian example: retreat and wait for winter.

uncertain of American support, Israel almost immediately accepted the Rogers proposal.

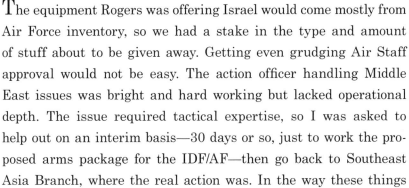

The equipment Rogers was offering Israel would come mostly from Air Force inventory, so we had a stake in the type and amount of stuff about to be given away. Getting even grudging Air Staff approval would not be easy. The action officer handling Middle East issues was bright and hard working but lacked operational depth. The issue required tactical expertise, so I was asked to help out on an interim basis—30 days or so, just to work the proposed arms package for the IDF/AF—then go back to Southeast Asia Branch, where the real action was. In the way these things seem always to happen, 30 days became 60, which became "until the Christmas break," which became "until we can write a fitness report on you," and I walked out of the Building three years later, having spent the entire time as the Air Staff officer responsible for policy regarding Israel and the Arab Confrontation States—Egypt, Jordan, Syria, and Lebanon. It was a better than average issue and I tried hard to understand it. Among other steps I took to add insight, I enrolled in the Armed Forces Institute's correspondence course, History of the Middle East, enjoyable off-duty reading that taught me a good bit.

In working the arms release package, I began to meet the other players in town, in and outside the Pentagon, who could influence the issue. Quickly, it was my phone that began to ring when the Air Force was involved in any operational matter concerning Israel or its Arab neighbors. Without trying, I usurped responsibility from the officer I was supposed to be helping.

I did not handle this development well, a personal failing. I should have reached out to my colleague, gone the extra mile to keep him informed and productive. More often, I left him out, not wanting to be slowed down. He must have thought me not a team player, which was true. But it's combat that requires cooperation, the team never any good until well broken to the harness.

By contrast, decent staff work is nearly always the product of individual effort. Anyway, I was putting in the extra hours, I was doing the writing and briefing, and, selfishly, I wanted the credit—or blame, if I got it wrong. It made my colleague unhappy, but market forces were at work in the Air Staff, a competition where the fittest survived.

Regarding the Arab-Israeli conflict, there seemed few serviceable answers, including the generally held view we should do everything possible to keep the "peace process" on track. No "process" substitutes for actual peace, which often comes only after a conflict has been allowed to burn out, to reach an outcome. Anyway, many factors, including not least domestic politics, combined to make it virtually impossible to wash our hands of the matter and, since we hadn't figured out how to fix it, we kept flogging that broken-down nag, the peace process. With level distribution of blame and obliged to pick sides, my inclination was to root for Israel. I admired the IDF/AF, whose performance at the outset of the Six-Day War showed what air forces, operating independently, could do. Besides, I quickly acquired Israeli fighter pilot buddies.

One afternoon, shortly after my transfer to the Mideast Branch, the office door swung open and in walked a short, dark-haired civilian, a grin synchronized with the sparkle in his eye. With some graying and a few more pounds of waistline consolidation, this could be Israel's Santa Claus, if they ever switched to celebrating Christmas. The "civilian" turned out to be a colonel, the Israeli air attaché, his presence in the office therefore a trespass. Everybody knew military attachés were in the spy business. My office worked mostly on matters carrying a high security classification, some of the stuff lying open on desktops, and this guy had no business poking his nose in, unescorted. But where Joe Alon was concerned, the rules did not adhere well.

Born in 1928 at Kibbutz Beth Alpha, Joe Alon returned with his parents to Czechoslovakia, where the family got caught up in World

War II. Smuggled out, he spent the war years in England, going back afterward to look for his family. They were gone. Joe went to Israel and, in 1948, volunteered for the first IDF/AF pilot's course. He qualified in jets early and took part in all the combat operations of the new air force, rising quickly in the years when the outfit was small and everybody knew everybody, front and back. By 1955, he'd become commander of a fighter squadron. During the Six-Day War, he commanded the pilot-training school but still managed to fly a few combat sorties in the French trainer, the Fouga Magister. He made it to colonel in an air force not yet top-heavy with rank, but he would not make general, being not quite severe enough. Washington would be his last military assignment.

Joe was puckish, mischievous, the sort of kid who sprays spitballs around class. I liked him a lot. His wife, Dvora, was an Oriental Jew, airlifted with her family out of Yemen as part of the "infolding" after establishment of the Jewish state in 1948. She was famous in the IDF/AF for her hospitality. Over the next couple of years we went often to the Alon house in Chevy Chase, Maryland, celebrating Passover and other Jewish holidays there. Dvora produced a magnificent *cholent*, a stew tasty enough to make any dinner invitation the excuse to cancel other appointments.

It turned out I would be working with Joe Alon a lot. I just needed to figure out how to keep him from wandering uninvited through my office.

The Air Force had grave reservations about releasing the equipment Secretary Rogers had held out to Israel in return for ending the War of Attrition. The package contained some leading-edge stuff—jamming equipment used to disrupt SAM acquisition, tracking, and missile guidance; the Navy's Shrike missile, designed to home in on and blow up radars. The wizardry that made this gear effective was the product of an elaborate collection effort; few US officers could work up much enthusiasm about losing control of the information. The list also included a variety of advanced munitions like cluster bombs, canisters containing maybe 1,000 hand-grenade-like submunitions. Make no mistake, these were antipersonnel weapons, deadly against troops (or civilians) in the open, and the thought of handing them over to anyone other than our closest NATO allies made us uneasy.

But it didn't matter what the Air Force thought. The overriding national concern was what the Soviets might do. If they were compelled to up the ante along the Suez in order to save face, we'd almost certainly be involved in a direct confrontation. In view of the importance of a cease-fire, Air Force reservations about the arms package being offered to Israel carried little weight.

When it was finished in 1943, the Pentagon was the world's largest office building, quite a feat for a structure with only five stories above ground. It was intended to serve only temporarily as a military headquarters. Roosevelt thought it much too big for any reasonably sized peacetime military staff and hoped it would become a national archive after the war. Leslie Groves helped oversee early construction before moving on to the Manhattan Project. There was a wartime shortage of steel, so the building is mostly concrete, one of the reasons it's so short and squatty. (Another is that FDR wanted to preserve the view from Arlington Cemetery.) Concentric rings surround a courtyard, at its center a sort of hotdog stand— the aim point for Russian missiles.

My office was on the fourth floor, D Ring. Visitors mostly saw the well-decorated E Ring, front offices where senior officers and civilians had windows giving onto the outside world. If you wandered away from the high-rent district, the Building quickly became a maze of shoddy smallholdings, blind alleys, dead ends. But after a few months of pounding a beat, I got to know my way around, except perhaps in the basement, a rabbit warren where even pilots could lose their bearings. Down there, I memorized how to get to and from the three or four places I visited often, always starting from the same stairwell. If I had to explore the unknown, I asked for directions from the Purple Water Fountain, an all-purpose basement landmark for AOs working above ground.

In the Pentagon, the Air Force had its own zip code, 20330, proof positive of our independence from the Army.

❧

In September 1970, the Jordanian Army attacked Palestinian refugee camps, defeating Palestine Liberation Organization militants in heavy fighting. For the PLO, this was Black September. Later that month, Egypt's President Nasser died. Anwar Sadat, the moderate, Western-oriented vice president, moved up to replace him.

❧

With the arms package to Israel approved, I was asked to set up training for a cadre of Israeli officers. I arranged to do this at the Nellis Fighter Weapons School. Joe Alon and I traveled there to monitor classroom work. Five Israeli fighter pilots showed up in Las Vegas. The senior officer was Col. Jacob Agassi, chief of IDF/AF operations. In his mid-40s—old by their standards—he was a large man who gave off the impression of physical strength. In class, his questions were direct to the point of bluntness. Here was a guy who wouldn't beat you with finesse but could probably slap on a few more *g*'s than you'd like to pull.

The other four were field-grade officers, my age or younger. Each was remarkable. Amos Lapidot was solemn and cerebral, with a quiet confidence that inspired trust. Indeed, he would be a future commander of the IDF/AF (and later, head of the Technion, Israel's premier engineering school at Haifa). Ran Ronen, smart and competitive, was a fighter ace whose reputation for pugnacity made him stand out even in Israel's air force, where immoderate aggressiveness passed unnoticed. Avihu Ben-Nun was another MiG killer, indeed credited with downing one of the Russians in Egypt. He would succeed Lapidot as head of their air force, our future tours as respective air chiefs overlapping. The last officer, Avi Lanir, was a very young major who came across as an idealist. He had a sort of freshness, a purity reflected in probing questions for which there were no straightforward answers. But like the others, he was a battle-hardened veteran who had scored well, already commander of a Mirage squadron.

With Joe Alon, the seven of us had a splendid time in Las Vegas. I still had friends at Nellis from my Thunderbird days, and Israeli fighter pilots automatically had keys to the city. On one particularly memorable evening, we barbecued steaks at the home of Tom Gibbs, then flying slot with the team. Lapidot made a "small salad," a specialty of his. Actually, the salad was quite large, but he chopped at the pieces until they were pretty small. The others told me Agassi could eat a steak of any size, so I shopped for the largest in Las Vegas, maybe a pound and a half. Down it went, no problem.

With these Israeli airmen, I got a first taste of Israel's version of operational security, or OPSEC. OPSEC starts with the belief that it's a bad idea for the other guy to know *anything* about you. It's not simply a matter of denying knowledge of what the intelligence experts call EEI, or essential elements of information, like the location and fighting condition of your unit. OPSEC means keeping any kind of knowledge from the enemy. The Russians were notoriously careless in this regard (and we were not much better). We regularly harvested Russian campsites to produce a bonanza of information—discarded equipment, tin-can labels, love letters—leading to insights that can produce game-winning estimates. My new friends were at the exact polar extreme. Most fighter pilots don't talk a lot anyway, social interaction being a learned behavior, but these Israeli airmen went much further, making a fetish of concealment and dissimulation. Even their names were deceptive, though Joe Alon did tell me his real name after a few drinks, and after I took an oath not to repeat it. None of these guys used the proper identifier of their operating base, though I knew these bases and their names very well. They said "north base" or "middle base." None of them discussed the number of kills they were credited with, though I had a more-or-less complete database of combat records. Nevertheless, and despite their best efforts, I accumulated a fair amount of information simply by spending time with them, knowledge that helped with my duties.

In the early '70s, it was still necessary to log a few flying hours each month in order to receive flight pay. Various kinds of aircraft were kept at Andrews Air Force Base so flyers assigned to the Pentagon could maintain proficiency. Conventional pilots flew the T-29, a twin-engine prop job used in navigator training. Jet bomber, tanker, and transport pilots flew the T-39, a small twin-jet transport. A fleet of T-33s was available for fighter jocks.

Shortly after arriving in Washington, I took my flying records out to Andrews and checked in with the sleepy apparatchik who managed this program. He went through the forms carefully, looking, as it turned out, for some excuse to put me in the T-29 or T-39, the T-33 being by a wide margin the most popular proficiency aircraft. At length he admitted to finding no easy way to keep me out of the T-33. I was surprised there had been any doubt. It was bad enough to be back in the T-bird.

After a quick recurrency program I began requesting the occasional cross-country flight, the usual way to log the flying-hour requirement. I flew one such cross-country with Paul Kattu, who had been Thunderbird lead the first year I applied for the team. Paul was a first-rate officer, a wonderful pilot, one of the all-time best Thunderbird leaders and a thoroughly nice guy, and here we were, trapped in the Pentagon—and the T-bird.

Returning with Paul to Washington on a clear night, I was in the backseat at altitude over rural Kentucky, the sky showing selected highlights. Paul asked if I recognized that lovely, small star cluster just overhead. Without thinking, I blurted out the name. But it was a no-notice test of character rather than knowledge. Paul had tricked me into showing off. I briefly considered digging the hole deeper by asking him to identify the Hyades, close by the Pleiades but less well-known, then wisely decided to pass. He'd already won.

Only a few months later, the T-birds were yanked out of Andrews, and everybody had to check out in the T-39. So, I got to fly airplanes cluttered up with passengers—still fun, maybe, but not why you signed up. In good time, the Air Force rightly decided to continue the flight pay for rated staff officers but stop the flying, which accounted for nearly all the cost. All proficiency aircraft disappeared from Andrews, and the four-hour-a-month flying requirement was lifted.

As we seemed settled for a while in the same spot, Ellie resumed work on a PhD in economics, attending classes at George Washington University. But in August 1971 the British ambassador turned up at the Treasury Department, asking that $3 billion held in their foreign exchange account be settled in gold. This development, along with rising domestic inflation, caused President Nixon to announce his New Economic Policy, part of which involved going off the gold standard and imposing a freeze on wages and prices. Nixon set up the Cost of Living Council to administer economic controls, meant to be relaxed gradually. Ellie took a job at the council, her first piece of business being to remove price controls on canned vegetables. Several tiers up, her boss was a former congressman from Illinois, Donald Rumsfeld, whose assistant was a future congressman from Wyoming, Dick Cheney.

Ellie's work was interesting and her responsibilities important, so we hired help to look after Brian. By now Mark was old enough to pretty much take care of himself, with the possible exception of the evening he and a couple of friends went to a Rolling Stones concert and inexplicably disappeared for some time afterward, causing Ellie to declare DEFCON 1. But Brian, an active child, needed supervision. Often he came home layered with mud after playing in a small creek behind houses across the street. Ellie's standing rule: after the third change of clothes, he stayed home. Fairfax County was building a new public library in the neighborhood, and Brian lent a hand. He became a fixture for construction workers, who let him carry materials around the site. Before the grand opening, he helped librarians stock the shelves—now recognized, a favored personality.

US 1, known hereabouts as Jeff Davis Highway, edged our neighborhood, carrying a full charge of fast-food outlets and a sprinkling of nicer spots. In one of its more upscale restaurants, I handed over a credit card to cover the cost of a family outing. Always until then we'd limited credit card usage to investment items—big-ticket, household stuff. Now, for the first time, we *consumed* and, shamelessly, signed for it. The action had no practical consequence, as I always settled the account in full each month and never paid interest on a balance. Still, I felt a little guilty.

In June 1971, at about my one-year point in the Pentagon, the *New York Times* began publishing a series of articles based on a 47-volume, top-secret study of US involvement in Southeast Asia commissioned by Robert McNamara. The so-called Pentagon Papers caused a stir, since they revealed the very considerable miscalculation, deception, and arrogance of US policy makers. It seemed to me there was not much new in the *Times* reporting (which "revealed," for instance, that we'd been bombing Laos for some time). However, the unfolding of the full story did indeed register— 7,000 pages of documents showing four presidents and their administrations lied systematically for more than 20 years. In its editorial of 17 June the *Washington Post* spoke of "the calculated misleading of the public, the purposeful manipulation of public opinion, the stunning discrepancies between public pronouncements and private plans."

New material or not, the Justice Department invoked national security grounds to bar further publication, getting an injunction subsequently tossed out by the Supreme Court. The government also indicted Daniel Ellsberg, a former State Department employee and a possible source of the *Times* material, on charges of espionage, theft, and conspiracy. The courts later dismissed the charges when it turned out that two government employees, E. Howard Hunt and G. Gordon Liddy, had broken into the office of Ellsberg's psychiatrist, looking for any kind of damaging evidence.

Almost no public-policy issue is an unequivocal, easy call. If facts and circumstances didn't support both sides of an argument, there wouldn't be much of an issue. But here, with the Pentagon Papers, we had pretty one-sided conditions, an unusual and interesting case that made everybody working in the executive branch look either corrupt or a complete idiot.

Perhaps an age of innocence was passing, but it seemed to me that from the publication of the Pentagon Papers onward, many knowledgeable Americans stopped believing what their government told them. And not just about the war.

The Arab-Israeli confrontation involved the Pentagon in issues that cut across service lines, so the Defense Department organized a central coordinating body, the Middle East Task Group (METG), with representation from the Joint Staff, the services, and other interested defense agencies. Officially, Jim Noyes, a political appointee in DOD's Office of International Security Affairs (the Pentagon's mini-State Department) chaired the METG, but Noyes's assistant, Maj. Gen. Devol "Rock" Brett, provided the muscle.

Rock Brett was a wonderful officer, a West Pointer with inspirational leadership qualities. He was smart enough, but his long suit was a winning personality and steel-reinforced integrity. His father, Army general George H. Brett, had been Douglas MacArthur's senior airman in the Philippines. MacArthur was not happy (perhaps unfairly) with the elder Brett and, after escaping to Australia, had him replaced by George Kenney. Kenney won MacArthur's confidence and went on to wage the outstanding air campaign that did so much to expel the Japanese from the Southwest Pacific.

Brig. Gen. Jim Allen was appointed Air Force member of the METG, and I was tagged to assist him as an add-on to my other AO responsibilities. A lean, smart West Pointer, Allen had flown P-51s in Korea, after which he spent considerable time in the bomber business. Simply a great officer, he would in the years ahead often be asked to work the thorniest Air Force problems. (For instance, he was detailed as special assistant to the chief of staff for B-1 deployment, when that program was especially troubled.) He ended up a four-star, running Military Airlift Command (MAC). I was very impressed to be working directly for him, and he seemed to like me.

General Eisenhower started the Pentagon Officers Athletic Club when he served briefly as Army chief of staff after World War II. I joined immediately and found it a sanity preserver. I tried to go down every day around noon for some exercise and a shower, which got me back in the mood to work into the evening. Nobody in my office played handball. Racquetball, which I denounced as a sissy sport, was all the rage. With no choice, I switched and soon got great enjoyment from the game. Not so physically punishing as handball, racquetball nevertheless put a premium on fitness, and in level competition you found out who really wanted to win. As I got to know Rock Brett in connection with staff work for the Middle East Task Group, I learned he favored squash, so I took up the game and soon played well enough to give him company. But I never got very good at squash, a game with disproportionate rewards for skill, as opposed to determination.

Brett lived near me in Virginia's Mount Vernon District and soon was telephoning for an occasional ride to work. We carpooled in my small sports car, a Datsun 240Z, perfect for the fighter pilot who couldn't afford Italian iron.

Early in 1972, President Nixon visited China, a gesture that caught everyone off guard and one that nearly justified his presidency. Against the background of the continuing Sino-Soviet split, this sudden move strengthened our position with the Russians and allowed for a general reduction of tensions. The most important manifestation of the thaw came in May, when Nixon and Brezhnev signed the Antiballistic Missile (ABM) Defense Treaty and the interim agreement limiting strategic offensive arms, SALT I. These agreements restricted deployment of missile defenses and froze the number of strategic ballistic missile launchers at existing levels, an acknowledgement that the Russians had achieved nuclear parity. Thus began a period of détente, a relaxation of the Cold War that would last until 1979.

In the spring of 1972, when Hanoi launched an offensive across the 17th parallel, we responded by resuming bombing in the North, at the same time offering to renew negotiations. Seemingly endless talking followed, but by October, a draft agreement was on the table, calling for a cease-fire in place, unilateral withdrawal of US forces, and the return of our POWs. In the days leading up to the 1972 presidential election, Secretary of State Henry Kissinger announced, "peace is at hand." But South Vietnam's President Nguyen Van Thieu, who had been excluded from the negotiations, decided he couldn't sign an agreement allowing perhaps 200,000 NVA regulars to stay in his country as we left. After Nixon swamped George McGovern in the presidential race, we tried to get the Hanoi delegation to withdraw their troops from the South, but they balked, walking out of the talks. To pressure the North and reassure the South, Nixon ordered Operation Linebacker II, the so-called Christmas Bombing, a round-the-clock pounding in which we used B-52s in the North for the first time.

During the first three days of Linebacker II, we lost nine B-52s. Three were shot down the first night, this being regarded for some reason as an acceptable loss rate. None were lost the second night, seeming to validate our tactics. Alarms sounded when six B-52s went down the third night. By this time, Jim Allen was working at

SAC headquarters and was tasked to explain the losses and make recommendations. He called me and some others he'd known at the Pentagon, and we flew out to Omaha. It was pretty straightforward. They'd been using the same attack plan every night, the rigidity springing from SAC's ossified planning process. The SAM shooters quickly figured out the stereotyped headings, altitudes, and formations. It was World War II all over again. We couldn't have planned it better if we wanted to get rid of surplus B-52s.

They didn't need our help at SAC. By the time we got there, Jim Allen had already solved the problem and directed more flexible tactics. The B-52 loss rate dropped dramatically, but the North showed no sign of yielding. Negotiations were restarted, and Nixon unilaterally stopped the bombing after 12 days. Subsequently, Henry Kissinger and North Vietnam's Le Duc Tho signed the Paris Agreement, including provisions for a cease-fire, total withdrawal of US troops, and release of 591 American POWs. No mention was made of NVA formations operating south of the DMZ, an omission that sealed Saigon's fate. (Thieu was told to take it or leave it.) Together, Kissinger and Tho won the Nobel Peace Prize, which Kissinger accepted without a show of embarrassment. Tho declined the honor, pointing out "peace has not yet really been established in Vietnam."

It's unlikely an Air Force officer in the operations career field will achieve authoritative depth on a political-military issue, but the problem I was working, the Arab-Israeli confrontation, stayed center stage, and it was nearly impossible not to learn a little about the region and its politics. Moreover, I continued my off-duty reading about the Middle East, the resulting insights useful in working contemporaneous staff papers.

Gradually, I met many of the personalities involved. A more or less constant stream of Israeli visitors passed through Washington, with rounds of official and unofficial entertainment at the

Israeli Embassy and Joe Alon's home. During this period, former IDF chief Yitzhak Rabin served as Israel's ambassador. Dour, deep voiced, slow of speech, Rabin seemed to regard Washington with an offhand distaste. When I navigated embassy receiving lines, Rabin's wife, Leah, kept watch over my shoulder to make sure she missed no one of importance.

Rabin returned to Israel in 1973 and became prime minister after Golda Meir was forced out in the recrimination that followed the Yom Kippur War. In the run-up to elections in 1977, Israeli newspapers said that, as IDF chief, Rabin had lost his nerve just before the kickoff of the Six-Day War and Moshe Dayan had to be brought in as minister of defense to stiffen the backbone. Nevertheless, when Rabin resigned just before the election, he did so because Leah, as rumored, had maintained an overseas bank account in violation of Israeli law.

In the Israeli Embassy, Joe Alon's immediate boss was an Army two-star, Motta Gur, a brilliant officer who as a teenager had been active in underground operations against the British. During the 1948 War of Independence, he served in a special commando unit; in the interwar period, he dropped behind Arab lines to conduct raids. By 1967, he commanded the Parachute Brigade, leading troops that liberated the Old City of Jerusalem. His phrase, "The Temple Mount is in our hands," broadcast by radio on 8 June 1967, is famous in Israel, memorializing the realization of a centuries-old Jewish ambition to return to this holy place.[2]

Like Rabin, Gur's talents were not challenged by his Washington duties. When first led into his office, I found him composing

---

2 In 1974, when Rabin was again named prime minister, he made Gur the IDF chief of staff. In this position, Gur helped plan the Entebbe Raid. Following his retirement from the army, Gur served in Labor cabinets as minister of health and deputy minister of defense. His own poor health kept him from attaining even higher political office and led to his early death, perhaps a suicide.

memoirs. He autographed and handed me a copy of his book for children, *Azeet, Paratrooper Dog*. The flyleaf tells the story:

> Azeet is a very special kind of dog, and no task is too difficult for her. She is dropped by parachute from an airplane to search for a young couple lost in enemy desert. She is fitted with oxygen tank and diving helmet to assist in the search for some frogmen who are overdue from their harbor mission. Her sensitive nose leads her to friend or foe—or to buried land mines—as if with a magnet. She follows vocal commands instantly, and when her master is injured in a desert raid, she finds her way back alone through enemy lines to bring help for him.
>
> In the burning heat of the desert or in the snows of Mount Hermon's wintry slopes Azeet serves unfailingly, and the daredevil members of the Israeli paratroop command know they can depend on her always. They all love Azeet and would gladly share their last drop of water with her. They know that with this faithful dog at their side it is easy to face the dangers that loom anew every day.
>
> Azeet repeatedly demonstrates her extraordinary sensory powers, her unflinching courage, and her canny intelligence. Readers will be filled with admiration for this wonderful dog who was a member of the army that has captured the imagination of the world.

❧

On 17 June 1972, police apprehended burglars inside Democratic Party headquarters in the Watergate apartment complex. In July, Jane Fonda visited Hanoi and was photographed wearing a helmet at an antiaircraft artillery site.

❧

My first trip to Israel sprang from their request for US help in building an aircraft they had under development, the Kfir, or Lion Cub. It was a knockoff of the French Mirage V. Israel had managed illicitly to obtain engineering drawings to get the project started. Now they wanted to install a US engine, the J-79 of F-104 and F-4 fame. DOD had to come up with a position on whether we should make the engine available. I was asked to go to Israel to look at the project as part of a team headed by Rock Brett.

In Israel, government officials took us into the factory where the first two Kfirs, test models not powered by the J-79, were nearing completion. We went in at night, after factory workers had gone home, the Israelis not wanting their own people to know outsiders were being shown the program. As if in a morgue at midnight, we examined the carcasses of these two unfinished aircraft—harsh, high-powered lamps throwing light into our corner of an immense and otherwise empty hangar.

This trip introduced me to many senior Israelis. I meet Gen. Moti Hod, the air force commander responsible for their success in the Six-Day War. We got along well. He offered me a ride in one of their operational Mirages. I jumped at the chance. At first, Brett said OK, then disappointed by phoning the request back to the Pentagon, where higher-ups (predictably) denied it.

At any rate, our trip was all form and no substance. The Israelis wanted the J-79 and had the political clout to get it.

September 1972 was a different sort of Black September, as Palestinian terrorists murdered 11 Israeli athletes at the Munich Olympic Games. Later in the year, Egypt's President Sadat expelled Soviet military advisers from what, at the time, was their only substantial deployment outside the Warsaw Pact.

Nineteen seventy-two was the year Frances Fitzgerald published *Fire in the Lake*, David Halberstam, *The Best and the Brightest*. After New Year's, the Supreme Court ruled, in Roe v. Wade, that a woman's right to have an abortion was protected by the Constitution.

Promotion in the Air Force was based on service. At each rank, a certain period of "time in grade" made an officer eligible for the next higher grade, putting him "in the zone" for promotion. As we climbed the ranks, getting promoted became statistically more difficult. That is, at successively higher grades a smaller percentage of those eligible in the zone were selected. From captain (later, major) on up, a few officers were promoted early, "from below the zone." To date, I'd been promoted on time; that is, when first eligible in the primary zone of service—certainly not early. In fact, considering my youthful exuberance, I'd quite likely been at the margins for due-course, on-time promotion. Now, at the Pentagon and with the exposure that came with working a high-profile issue, I was for the first time promoted early, from below the zone. In fact, I received two such promotions, not bad for a three-year tour. I made lieutenant colonel as soon as I was eligible for early selection and had worn the silvered devices of this rank for only four months when my name appeared on the list for promotion to full colonel. This elevator ride sounds faster than it was because the Air Force got two increments of happiness out of each promotion. First, the service announced the promotion; then, eventually, it became effective, often after protracted delay. With each of these two promotions earned in the Pentagon, I waited more than a year to pin on the new insignia of rank.

I was also selected to attend the National War College. The Air Force tapped only a small fraction of officers for senior service school, so this was a nice compliment—the more so because, like Armed Forces Staff College, National War College was a joint school and therefore a somewhat more esteemed choice.

In February 1973, Nixon announced the end of the draft and the adoption of the only feasible alternative, an all-volunteer force. Though he had promised as early as his 1968 campaign to end conscription, it was a series of lawsuits that finally forced the president's hand. Section 20 of the law regulating the draft provided for a 90-day waiting period between notification and induction, a proviso the government had ignored, considering its inclusion a legislative mistake. As a consequence, a rather large number of so-called Section 20 lawsuits found their way into courts all across the country. At length Justice William O. Douglas issued an injunction supporting Section 20, according to legend pinning the paperwork to a tree near the Cascade Range campsite where he was hiking.

I was very uneasy about doing away with conscription. We were on the edge of a revolution in military capabilities, based mainly on the increased accuracy of air-delivered munitions, and that development alone might ease our way to, or even mandate armed forces composed entirely of long-service volunteers. But we didn't know this for sure. In truth, we'd been compelled by the empty-headedness of our Vietnam politics to adopt the all-volunteer force. Anyway, the idea of some kind of public service, including military service, as an aspect of healthy citizenship, held strong appeal for me.

In April, the Watergate crisis heated up, with Nixon getting resignations from two top aides, H. R. Haldeman and John Ehrlichman, and firing John Dean as White House counsel.

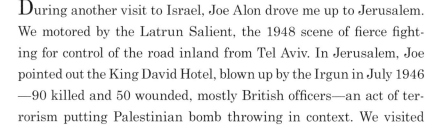

During another visit to Israel, Joe Alon drove me up to Jerusalem. We motored by the Latrun Salient, the 1948 scene of fierce fighting for control of the road inland from Tel Aviv. In Jerusalem, Joe pointed out the King David Hotel, blown up by the Irgun in July 1946 —90 killed and 50 wounded, mostly British officers—an act of terrorism putting Palestinian bomb throwing in context. We visited the Western Wall and, standing virtually on top of it, the Al-Aqsa Mosque, these two structures among the world's holiest places.

We drove on to the Dead Sea and, toward its southern end, dismounted to take a cable car up to Masada. Joe told me that, as part of their graduation exercise, officer candidates about to be commissioned in the Armored Corps spent a night on top this rugged mesa. Round the campfire, they retold the story of how Jewish diehards sought refuge here and held out for years while the Romans built a causeway that would eventually bring the fortress under assault. Finally, the prospect of certain Roman victory approaching, the Zealots drew straws to see which of them would kill the others, the last ones committing suicide rather than surrender.

The cadets slept on this story and next morning raised their hands to be sworn in as tank platoon leaders. Their subsequent performance in combat had become a legend. These guys rode around with the tank hatch open, sitting up high and exposed, so better to see what was going on.[3]

On each return to Israel, I renewed my acquaintance with Agassi, Lapidot, Ronen, Ben-Nun, and Lanir. One evening, Avi Lanir and I dined alone at Shaul's, the famous Yemeni restaurant in Jerusalem, where the *cholent* was good but not up to Dvora Alon's standard.

Up in the front office, General Ryan's exec was Lt. Col. Mike Carns, a graduate of the first class produced by the Air Force Academy. One day Carns accompanied Ryan to the White House, where the service chiefs had gone to brief the president on some issue. Afterward, Carns came to see me. Apparently, the chief of naval operations had taken the opportunity to trot out the latest Navy marketing effort, Relevant Power. Our Navy was always there, on scene, the only force ready to intervene quickly. Sure, the other services were important, but mostly in the mopping-up phase. Carns told me he'd never seen the chief so angry. He wanted me to prepare a paper for use at the JCS meeting the next day, showing how the Air Force was just maybe "relevant" in the Middle East. He'd come directly to me because there wasn't much time.

Like many AOs, I kept a shaving kit in the office, and this was one of the nights I didn't go home. Naturally, my paper sparked plenty of interest in the layers of supervision between me and the chief—not that anybody wanted to fiddle with it, but they did want to take a look, sign off, make sure they were not left out, all of which took time I didn't have. Early morning, Carns showed up in the office asking for the paper. By now, a handful of colonels huddled around my desk, "helping" me. Someone told Carns the paper

---

3 This tactic was abandoned following the Yom Kippur War, which saw the destruction of so much Israeli armor.

wasn't fully coordinated. He asked, "Is Tony happy with it?" When I nodded assent, he picked up the paper and without further ado took it to the chief, an act of generosity I wouldn't forget.

❧

What was the JCS view on such-and-such an issue? The question came up regularly, and consequently there was a structured, formal process for establishing a JCS position. The Joint Staff worked up a proposal, often with action officers from the service staffs assigned to draft parts of the position paper. The topic was scheduled to appear on the JCS agenda. Every service AO regarded it as a disaster if the proposed JCS position differed much from the views of his own chief. Naturally, it was a whole lot easier if your chief's ideas were in the first draft of the paper. When the services differed on a matter, the elbowing for position could be vigorous.

I quickly got acquainted with the AOs from each service who worked Middle East issues. My Marine Corps counterpart was a major named Bud McFarlane. I didn't know it at the time, but Bud's father had been a congressman, Bud himself had graduated from Annapolis high in his class, and he was in the process of establishing a great record of public service that would culminate in President Reagan choosing him as his national security adviser. All I knew was he was trustworthy and turned in clear, well-organized prose. OK, he worked the Marine Corps problem, but he managed to do it in a way that didn't threaten the rest of us. By contrast, our Army and Navy counterparts were much less open-minded. So, when necessary, Bud and I conferred off to the side and divided the work, ignoring assignments made by the Joint Staff and getting back quickly with quality inputs that baked our views into the first version of a joint position. The others then had to try to pry us out.

I like to think Bud McFarlane and I put the country's interest first, but I could see that many able officers pushed their own service's parochial view and were rewarded for doing so. The processes at work in the big Pentagon bureaucracy were Darwinian, and that was fine. We just needed to move beyond the tribal-warfare stage.

In early 1973 I accompanied General Hod, who was retiring from his post as commander of the IDF/AF, on a farewell trip through the United States. He and I spent a lot of time flying around the country in the back end of a T-39. He visited several USAF bases, including Langley, where he met with Spike Momyer, then in his last months as commander of Tactical Air Command.

The two were scheduled to meet privately, and I should have been left sitting outside, but Hod insisted I come in to audit the meeting. The episode had an otherworldly aspect, Momyer turning it into a monologue on how he'd been thwarted in Vietnam. Spike fancied himself the world's smartest, most seasoned air tactician. He yielded pride of place to no one, but cleared a small spot for Hod, whom he tacitly acknowledged might also know a thing or two about air combat.

As we left Momyer's office, we passed a rogues' gallery, portraits of former TAC commanders. Hod paused, remarking that Momyer's likeness would soon join the rest. "Yes," Spike said, "and when I'm gone, there'll be no one left with any real experience in using theater air forces in battle." Momyer was a great airman, and I suppose he meant this as a compliment to Hod, someone with shared expertise that set them apart. In the event, Momyer would be succeeded by Gen. Bob Dixon, who would be followed by Gen. Bill Creech. Each would head TAC for five years or so. Neither would show any sign of uneasiness about his ability to lead air forces in combat.

I left the Pentagon in the summer of 1973, taking a week off to do long-neglected house repairs before my War College class started up. The Senate Watergate hearings were under way, so I carried a portable radio as I climbed the ladder to apply a fresh coat of paint. On 16 July, the committee's minority counsel, Fred Thompson, asked former White House aide Alexander Butterfield, "Are you aware of the installation of any listening devices in the Oval Office of the president?"

It seemed for a moment as though Nixon might be finished before I got the house painted, but he floundered for 13 more months.

❧

Joe Alon was murdered in the early hours of Sunday, 1 July 1973. Coming home from a social event late at night, he left Dvora at the front door and went to put the car away. He was shot five times from bushes next to the garage. It was a thoroughly professional job, and the killer was never caught.

Still a young man. Only 43 years old at the time of his death.

I thought about a recent trip with Joe, again to Las Vegas. I'd rented a car and driven to the top of Mount Charleston, an enchanted place where, in late spring, we stood in dirty snow and looked down across shimmering desert. I'd meant to repay him with a view perhaps not entirely unlike the one he'd given me from Masada's ramparts.

Gen. George Brown, nominated to become the Air Force's new chief of staff, authorized the use of his aircraft to fly Joe back to Israel. I was detailed to accompany the body and take Dvora and the three daughters home.

It was hot in Israel, and Jews don't embalm. They buried Joe quickly in a plain wooden box. I found myself preferring their way of doing this business.

The evening following interment, Dvora hosted a large gathering at the home she and Joe owned in Herzliya. All my friends from the IDF/AF were there. Joe had shopped in the States and purchased air-conditioning equipment for the house, but it was not yet installed, so the doors and windows were thrown open. At a certain point, I was getting some air, standing in the front door with Ezer Weizman, whose uncle, Chaim Weizmann, had been president of Israel and who himself would hold that office one day. Ezer Weizman had been part of Israel's air force from its beginnings, commanding it from 1958 to 1966. He still flew a coal-black Spitfire in annual Air Force Day celebrations. We were deep in conversation when he stopped abruptly: "Uh-oh, here comes Dayan. I have to leave."

It turned out Weizman's wife was the sister of Moshe Dayan's first wife. Because Dayan had traded for a new model, Mrs. Weizman would not occupy the same house with him. The Weizmans left the party.

One way to understand Israel is to remember it's tiny, more like a village than a country.

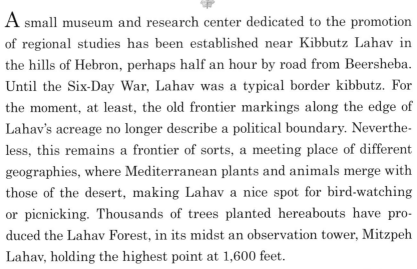

A small museum and research center dedicated to the promotion of regional studies has been established near Kibbutz Lahav in the hills of Hebron, perhaps half an hour by road from Beersheba. Until the Six-Day War, Lahav was a typical border kibbutz. For the moment, at least, the old frontier markings along the edge of Lahav's acreage no longer describe a political boundary. Nevertheless, this remains a frontier of sorts, a meeting place of different geographies, where Mediterranean plants and animals merge with those of the desert, making Lahav a nice spot for bird-watching or picnicking. Thousands of trees planted hereabouts have produced the Lahav Forest, in its midst an observation tower, Mitzpeh Lahav, holding the highest point at 1,600 feet.

The Joe Alon Center, including the Museum of Bedouin Culture, rises on the hillside halfway between the kibbutz and the mitzpeh. It's built of stone quarried from the region and stands at the hub of tracks leading into the forest in all directions.

Logbook: Pentagon, 1970–73

T-33	T-39
94.1	159.4

Chapter 2

War College

For to win one hundred victories in one hundred battles is not the acme of skill. To subdue the enemy without fighting is the acme of skill. Thus, what is of importance in war is to attack the enemy's strategy.

—Sun Tzu, *The Art of War*

Each year about 140 students attended National War College, located at Fort Lesley J. McNair in Washington, DC. A quarter of the seats were reserved for civilians, mostly from State and CIA. The idea was to include everyone who might have a voice in interagency discussions about national security, so other agencies, like Treasury or the FBI, also sent a sprinkling of students. Some of my civilian classmates went on to notable careers. One or two became ambassadors. But the emphasis was military. Each of the three service departments got about 35 places each, all given to colonels (or Navy captains), or lieutenant colonels certain soon to be colonels. In the Class of 1974 were three other future Air Force four-stars. Monroe Hatch would end up our vice chief of staff, John Shaud would become chief of staff at NATO's Supreme

Headquarters Allied Powers Europe (SHAPE), and Jim McCarthy would finish his active service as deputy commander in chief, US European Command.

The POWs came home from Hanoi in early 1973, and by fall many had recovered sufficiently to attend school. Four came from the Air Force: Fred Cherry, Fred Crow, Dick Dutton, and Sam Johnson. Sam was an ex-Thunderbird slot man, bagged taking an F-105 across Hanoi. He went on to become a long-term US congressman from Texas.

Also in the class was a good friend and future major general, Tom Swalm. Tom had led the Thunderbirds early in the F-4 era. I saw him do several shows, a particularly memorable one at Washington's Dulles Airport, where we lost the right wingman, Joe Howard, because of flight-control failure. Swalm grew up in Southern California, helping invent or perfect a number of only mildly hazardous beach games. He'd gone on to be a track star and Olympic-level volleyball player at the University of Oregon. At a minimum, he was a competitor, a Jedi knight, a wonderful airplane driver, certainly one of the best formation leaders ever. If anything, his performance on the ground was even better. He possessed, for a fighter pilot, unusually well-developed social skills. Supposedly, tigers and lions are close enough genetically to mate and produce offspring. But tigers are solitary; lions, social animals. Tom was a lion.

Fort McNair was also the site of another senior military institution, the Industrial College of the Armed Forces (ICAF), a school for logisticians (our name: "shoe clerks"). In 1973–74, NWC played ICAF in eight sports, splitting four and four. Tom captained the volleyball team, trying unsuccessfully to show me how to leave the floor to spike the ball. I redeemed myself by helping win the first-ever racquetball competition between the schools.

Over the years, I lost track of most of the civilians and members of other services in the Class of '74. I do remember another ex-POW, this one from the Navy, a young, skinny, physically beat-up

John McCain, the junior man of the class. Only a lieutenant commander (equivalent to major) when he showed up, John pinned on commander rank during the school year.

⚜

Fort McNair was an island of calm staked out on the Anacostia River, in one of the capital's grimmest neighborhoods. It featured a parade ground, put to peacetime use as a par-three golf course; a row of stately Georgian homes along the riverbank; and the college itself, a splendid red-brick dating from 1918. For many years, it served as the Army War College, but that institution was removed to Carlisle Barracks, Pennsylvania, when, after World War II, the need arose for a joint school. Class pictures dating back to 1947 adorned the halls, the old boys (and now, girls) including many distinguished personages.

The National War College concerned itself with national strategy—how to formulate it, how to embed it in policy, how to execute it. We pursued these themes in readings, lectures, and seminar sessions. The key questions: What is the national interest? How is it best served? These are abstract topics, mushier than they would seem at first, and we got a daily dose of prominent speakers, military and civilian, to help us with inquiries. But, reduced to essentials, the message was that a great power works its will in many ways: economic, diplomatic, social, political, cultural, even moral or ethical. It was not a hard sell. Military professionals are the first to understand that we needn't settle every international dispute by the bayonet.

In fact, it was too simple an issue and, in addition, not germane. Very few of those attending NWC would ever make a meaningful contribution to the Washington dialogue about national security. The roles, missions, and functions of the services—who does what on the battlefield and how these activities might be more efficiently directed, integrated, and supported—would be an interesting study topic, and potentially more fruitful, in the sense that graduates might expect, in later years, to have some influence on the matter.

Of course, "roles and missions" would be controversial, likely to divide and separate a student body meant to be joined and unified. But if students worked together on answers then, over many years, a sort of senior-level consensus might emerge that could make it possible to rationalize the way we organize to provide security to our country at reasonable cost. At a minimum, some of our future generals and admirals might begin to understand why having, for instance, three armies and five air forces is a costly and damaging way to organize, a kind of subversion of the very national interest we are supposed to serve.

We might have started with the story of Lt. Gen. Leslie J. McNair, the man whose name was on the installation we came to every day. One of the Army's most promising officers, McNair was the senior officer killed by friendly fire in World War II. Eighth Air Force did it, dropping the bomb that exploded in his foxhole near Saint-Lô, in Normandy.

In October 1973, the Yom Kippur War broke out. Overestimating their ability to handle Egyptian and Syrian air defenses, Israel's air force lost 40 aircraft, about 12 percent of its prewar combat inventory, in the first two days.[4] Avi Lanir was shot down over Syrian-held territory in the Golan Heights, parachuting from his aircraft and hitting the ground safely. The Israelis believe he was captured, tortured, finally killed. Eventually, Israeli forces clawed their way back to a tactical success. But, like Tet for us, the Yom Kippur War was a psychological, even a cultural defeat for Israel.

During my stay at NWC, I earned an advanced degree in international relations, attending evening classes managed by George Washington University. To get ahead in the Air Force, officers must obtain a master's degree, and this was an effortless way to do

---

4 In just 19 days of conflict, the IDF/AF lost 109 aircraft, fully 35 percent of its prewar strength.

it, though George Washington administered written examinations, an aspect of education we had sensibly abandoned in connection with the NWC curriculum.

✿

Vice President Spiro Agnew was allowed to plead no contest to charges of income tax evasion in October 1973, on condition that he resign. President Nixon replaced him with House Minority Leader Gerald Ford.

In the Saturday Night Massacre, Attorney General Elliot Richardson and his deputy, William Ruckelshaus, resigned rather than follow Nixon's direction to fire Archibald Cox, the special prosecutor investigating the Watergate scandal. Solicitor General Robert Bork, later a celebrated Supreme Court nominee, did follow orders, giving Cox his walking papers, but this was the beginning of the end for Nixon.

✿

One of the great things about National War College was the chance for an extended visit to some important part of the world. The class split into five groups, each going a different direction. From start to end, the trip lasted a full three weeks. My group visited India, Pakistan, Afghanistan, Iran, Saudi Arabia, Jordan, Israel, and Egypt. At every stop, we met top government leaders. I shook hands with Ali Bhutto, the soon-to-be assassinated president of Pakistan. In Tehran, I met the soon-to-be deposed Shah of Iran. I drank bitter Arab tea in King Faisal's ceremonial tent and, following his lead, tossed the dregs into the pile of a carpet worth more than our house in Northern Virginia. Golda Meir welcomed us to Israel. Like her country, she radiated energy from a diminutive body. We crossed the Allenby Bridge and entered the Hashemite Kingdom, motoring up an attractive canyon toward Amman and stopping en route for yet another of those self-service meals of lamb and rice we impolitely called a "goat grab," eaten (to be sure!) with the right hand. We followed the Nile upriver to meet Anwar Sadat at his winter residence, passing through physical protection that would fail, in the end, to keep him alive. Only in New Delhi, where Indira Gandhi was upset with the United States for some reason, did we not meet a head of state.

On 28 January 1974, orders were cut rating me a command pilot, the more-or-less automatic upgrade at 15 years of rated service. I bought new wings, with a wreath around the star. On 1 March, in the NWC library, I put on the silver eagles of a full colonel.

Chapter 3

1st Fighter Wing

I would recommend a solo flight to all prospective suicides. It tends to make clear the issue of whether one enjoys being alive or not.

—T. H. White, *England Have My Bones*

Following War College graduation, I was assigned to the 1st Fighter Wing, located at MacDill Field, Tampa, Florida, as assistant deputy commander for operations (ADO). My job was to help the operations deputy, Col. Craven C. "Buck" Rogers, supervise the wing's four flying squadrons. A hard-charging, inexhaustible West Pointer, Buck possessed strong fighter credentials and had served a tour in officer assignments, so he knew something about manipulating the personnel system. I admired him but found it tough keeping up. An early riser, I was at work by 7:00 a.m., but I liked having dinner with the family. I figured 12 hours was a long enough duty day in peacetime. Up to this posting, I'd been able to watch the boss depart, but Buck never seemed to go home. I quickly gave up and just left him there, a move he countered many times by calling me into his office for an evening of interminable discussion, usually concerning how we might shuffle aircrews around the wing. We left no alternative unexplored.

I was an assistant deputy commander for operations for only a few months, but long enough to formulate an important career-management principle: avoid any assignment with two modifiers in the job title.

The 1st Wing was what we called a replacement training unit, or RTU. We checked out pilots in the F-4 and prepared them for follow-on assignment to operational squadrons. Normally, such instruction took place at a combat crew training base, like Luke, but the manpower demands of Vietnam were so great that regular operational wings like the 1st changed missions to become RTUs.

Our flying squadrons were famous, old-line units, especially the "Hat-in-the-Ring" 94th, Eddie Rickenbacker's squadron. I was proud to wear the patch of the 27th, Frank Luke's outfit and the oldest fighter squadron in the Air Force, having flown cloth-covered Spads and Sopwith Camels in 1917. I checked out in the F-4 and, after four-and-a-half years, I was back flying fighters.

On August 8, 1974, Nixon resigned and was succeeded by Gerald Ford, who pardoned the former president within a month.

The F-4 had been the premier Air Force fighter for all the time I'd been out of the cockpit, and even before—the true third-generation replacement for the Century Series. Had I been patient after leaving the Thunderbirds, I could have checked out in the Phantom en route to Vietnam, but I was in a hurry to get there. Also, a hard-core single-engine, single-seat guy, I regarded the jet as weighed down with excess engines and people.

Because of our own shortsightedness in the years when the tactical force was trying to be a lesser Strategic Air Command, the Air Force had dropped the ball on fighter acquisition. As losses mounted in Vietnam, it became clear we needed a replacement fighter but had no time to develop one from scratch. We therefore attached ourselves to the Navy's F-4 program, at first buying the F-4C, incorporating only modest changes to the Navy standard F-4B, and later the D and E models, each with incremental improvements of our own design. At MacDill, the 1st Wing was equipped with F-4Es. In its final Air Force configuration, the E mounted an internal 20 mm gun and movable slats on the wing's leading edges, modifications meant to compensate for deficiencies in missile performance and aircraft maneuverability.

The Phantom was meant for fleet air defense. Like all interceptors, it had to get off the deck, climb to altitude quickly and close on the target at high speed. A growth version of the J-79, the great General Electric engine we'd used in the F-104, was just perfect for this application, and the Navy put in two of them. Although it's an arguable point, I was convinced the twin-engine approach gave something away because of performance compromises involving weight, frontal area, and intake design. However, even I would admit it was comforting to have that second, "get me home" engine when flying over open water.

The jet also had a powerful radar that acquired and tracked targets and guided the Sparrow missile. Using proper technique for separating friendlies from hostiles, the pilot could shoot from beyond visual range (BVR), a new style of air-to-air warfare in which a target aircraft is fired on before it can be seen by the eyeball. But getting to firing parameters within the close tolerances required for BVR engagement could be a handful, so the Navy put in a second cockpit, with a back-seater, head down in the radar scope, helping the pilot manage intercept geometry.

This new BVR capability was what made the Phantom a third-generation fighter. It also created an upheaval in air-to-air tactics. The end of dogfighting had been predicted for years; indeed, that's why the Navy had left the gun out in early versions of the Phantom. But now the era of close-in, visual air combat might actually be coming to an end, since a pilot no longer needed to work his way around behind the target to train guns or ensure that I/R-guided missiles, like the current-generation Sidewinder, could see a good heat source.

Making allowance for missile performance—the Sparrow was a true "missile," as opposed to a "hittile"—the F-4 met its air-to-air design goals pretty well. In addition, it carried a respectable air-to-ground load, about twice the normal bomb tonnage of the World War II-era B-17. It could be considered the first genuine multirole fighter, able both to take on enemy interceptors and deliver air-to-ground ordnance on the same mission. The airplane was tough enough to withstand the beating of carrier-deck operations, rugged to the point of being muscle-bound, and clumsy by Air Force standards. We called it "Double Ugly" or "The Rhino." It flew like what it was, a big, heavy aircraft, but if the Air Force wanted elegant fighter designs, like the P-51 or F-86, it had only itself to blame.

Anyway, it beat flying a desk in the Pentagon.

MacDill was another of those multimove experiences, like George or Woodbridge. On arrival, our assigned quarters were not ready for occupancy, so we had furniture delivered to a small apartment on base, then packed up and moved again when the house was ready. By now, moving had become a second career, and I knew from experience that half a mile was about as bad as coast-to-coast.

But I couldn't complain; I was back on the flight line. The wing had access to open airspace over the Gulf of Mexico and a fine air-to-mud range nearby at Avon Park. Getting back into the swing of flying filled every day with pleasure. I savored new supervisory responsibilities. I'd always enjoyed being around airfields. Now I had a staff car and a license to poke my nose into any part of the operation. I spent every second I could away from the office, chasing seagulls off the runway at sunup, visiting the tower and mobile control van, keeping an eye on aircraft as they taxied out, armed, lined up, took off.

One blemish in a sea of good fortune: though I mentioned it to no one, I was not the airplane driver I wanted to be, in large part because the F-4 was a step-function increase in the complexity of various aircraft systems.

Take the ejection seat. The F-4 had a Martin-Baker rocket-powered ejection seat, a complicated, clunky design (the seat had more than 1,300 parts) that had nevertheless saved many lives because of its low-and-slow capability, a "must have" feature Navy pilots needed to survive a "cold" catapult shot off a carrier deck. Over the years, Martin-Baker improved performance until it got to "zerozero," which, in theory, meant you could eject at any airspeed or altitude, including in the parking lot, and walk away from it. But the seat was intricate, with lots of little, obscure details to check during preflight.

Like most fighter pilots, my preflight inspection seemed laidback, the rigor hidden from view. A practiced eye assessed the big picture even before arriving at the airplane. Was the flight line clean and squared away? What did the other aircraft look like? Was the crew chief at the jet to meet me? Were the aircraft records in good order? You might need to look at parts of the airplane or handle them during a walk-around inspection (you probably do not need to kick the tires), but the important question remained, is this thing ready to fly or not? If it was ready, I wanted to strap it on and go fly. The fight starts at the bottom rung of the ladder. I didn't like any delay on the way up to the cockpit for thorough examination of something like a complicated ejection seat—which the other guy, not me, was about to need.

This attitude works only if you really know what you're doing. Above all, flying is a matter of cunning, which starts with preparation. Always before, with the F-100 or F-104, my ground preparation had been, if anything, overly elaborate: academics, simulator, long hours of briefings, all carefully designed to ramp up understanding. Now a full colonel and therefore a person of some consequence, I was run through a superficial, senior-officer checkout. After all, I had other, more important, things to do. As a result, I never got comfortable with the aircraft systems, especially the ones that do the damage, the radar and fire-control systems, and the dance of fingers that must be automatic if you want to win, or even stay alive, in combat. I felt safe enough in the airplane, even judged I was still pretty good at things requiring only airmanship—routine flight operations, aerobatics, formation, instruments—but I was marginal at best when it came to using the jet for its intended purpose. In the simulated air engagements I fought, I was usually right at the point of racking up an undeniable video kill when I mashed down on the wrong button and had to start over at the beginning of the whole radar search, track, lock-on, and fire sequence—during which time I got smoked instead.

I made a note: if ever again called to fly in actual combat, I'd need to get out of the management business and go through regular crew training, starting from square one.

In the fall of 1974, someone in the Colonels' Group at the Pentagon called to say I'd been ticketed to become air attaché to Cambodia. I told him he must have the wrong phone number since I'd been at MacDill about four months, and, anyway, Cambodia was obviously falling off the edge of the known universe. There was no chance I, or anyone else, could get to Phnom Penh before the Khmer Rouge. I did not have a good listener at the other end of the line. This was a key job. The air attaché actually ran Cambodia's air force. We'd brought legendary air commando Heinie Aderholt out of retirement to supervise its reconstruction, and it was time to replace him with a new guy. It was an honor to be selected—blah, blah, blah—all this in the age-old tradition of the flesh peddler trying to keep the "stuckee" from slashing his wrists.

What actually happened was that Gen. Bob Dixon, the TAC commander, had inventoried his colonel supply and picked those he regarded as keepers, the ones with the right career profile and potential to become wing commanders in the near term. The rest (including me) he made available for reassignment. If I put the best face on it, I was perhaps too young to get a wing anytime soon. The luck of the draw had dealt me Cambodia. Preparation would take a year, starting with five months of French language training at the State Department's Foreign Service Institute, followed by intelligence training, and finishing with a checkout in the C-12, the prop-driven passenger aircraft used to support our ambassador in Phnom Penh. None of this made sense to me.

The double move at the beginning kept us from getting drapes up at MacDill. We'd ordered them, but they'd not yet arrived, Ellie having improvised by hanging bedsheets at the windows. We canceled the drape order. We'd moved the kids around some already (and would do so some more) but now, for the first time, we got negative feedback. Mark had discovered the (reciprocated) joys of the opposite sex and was unhappy about leaving Tampa. We were saved from outright mutiny only because he was graduating from high school and would soon leave for college anyway.

During the last days of our short stay at MacDill, I was sent out to Luke Field to investigate a particularly nasty accident. An F-4 with a student at the controls had collided with a T-38 "Aggressor," a pilot specially trained to mimic Soviet air tactics.[5] All involved were killed.

Following any major accident, the Air Force conducted two investigations: a safety investigation, and the one I was to do in this case, the so-called collateral investigation. We did safety investigations to find out quickly why an accident happened, not to apportion blame. We immunized witnesses and could use the conclusions and

---

5 Following our poor performance against the North Vietnamese Air Force, we had upgraded air combat training. Among other initiatives, we established a small number of Aggressor Squadrons, with pilots trained to fly Soviet aircraft, or small, hard-to-see jets like the T-38. They subsequently provided very valuable, realistic training.

recommendations for no purpose other than to improve safety. We considered the proceedings privileged and did not release findings to the public. In the separate collateral investigation that followed, we took testimony under oath and did make the findings available to the public and for use in disciplinary or administrative action.

Vigorous safety enforcement is of course essential but would be self-defeating if we confused human error with willful misconduct and criminalized it. In the 1930s, the Army Air Corps almost never found a pilot at fault in an accident. This was because accident investigation findings were usually attached to a "report of survey," the form used by the government to write off lost equipment. Holding the pilot responsible would have formed the basis for pecuniary liability. The threat of civil liability or even criminal charges hobbled early safety probes by making witnesses shy away from speaking frankly, or at all. But we have to know if someone has made a mistake so we can take immediate preventive action and not waste time chasing ghosts.

This system of twin investigations caused no end of trouble for the Air Force. In a litigious society, not everyone was happy we might learn something we couldn't disclose. In this context, tort lawyers were concerned with the dead, or their estates. The Air Force mourns its dead and cares deeply about grieving families, but the safety program is for the living. It seeks to keep them alive.

Col. Bob Russ, vice-commander of the 4th Wing at Seymour Johnson AFB, was running the safety investigation for the Luke mishap. I'd met Bob when he was flying F-101s at Bentwaters but did not know him well. An exceptionally able officer, Russ would end up a four-star, commanding TAC. When I got to Luke, he was winding down his investigation. There was a strict separation of the two inquiries, each supposed to develop its own conclusions, but I learned that Bob thought this was a "normal" accident, the kind of thing that comes along from time to time as part of the inherent risk of the flying business.

My collateral investigation reached the same conclusion.

Supervision had been good. The aircraft were properly equipped and flyable in accordance with applicable regulations. The flight crews were qualified. The training sequence leading up to the mishap was logical and well designed. Mission preparation before the accident sortie was adequate. The crews involved were in good physical shape, had been given an opportunity to get a night's sleep, had eaten breakfast. It just happened they were unlucky enough to be in airplanes trying to occupy the same airspace at the same time. Case closed, turn in the report, head back to MacDill.

Within a couple of days, I got a call from the TAC inspector general, who had heard some interesting gossip about this class of F-4 students at Luke. Had I looked into the personal life of the pilots? What about drug abuse? Wife swapping? In fact, I had not inquired. He told me to get my butt back out to Luke and ask the right questions, stupid. When I did, I uncovered a new landscape, filled with a variety of creepy-crawlies.

Maybe the Air Force's most important safety initiative is to insist that future commanders preside over safety and collateral investigations. If destined for high rank, colonels, at about the 17- or 18-year service point, are halfway into a career. A decade and a half behind them is a follow-on generation of lieutenants. The lesson of the Luke investigation: never assume you understand what that next generation is up to.

Logbook: MacDill, 1974–75

| F-4E | 108.5 |

Chapter 4

Council on Foreign Relations

I always wanted to be someone and now I realize I should have been more specific.

—Lily Tomlin

In April 1975, I reported to the State Department's Foreign Service Institute to begin a course in conversational French, the instruction as good as any I'd ever received. I spent six hours a day with a native French speaker and listened to tapes at night and on weekends. No reading or writing, just straight conversation, more or less the way human beings learn their mother tongue. Two weeks into the five-month French course, Phnom Penh fell to the Khmer Rouge. I rang up my detailer at Colonel Assignments to say, "OK, genius, now what?" His reply: "Just keep learning French," very knowing, as though there was an advanced game plan already in motion. In a few days, I got new orders posting me as attaché to Saigon—also an obvious nonstarter. When our helicopters lifted the last Americans off the embassy roof on 29 April, it looked like I might run them out of jobs requiring some grasp of French.

I checked in again with Colonel Assignments about midway

through the course, maybe two and a half months in, a Thursday, midmorning. He had nothing for me. Twenty minutes later, he called back, agitated, pulling me out of class. Could I go to New York City tomorrow for an interview?

Each year the Air Force nominated a colonel for assignment as Military Fellow at the Council on Foreign Relations, a high-profile group of business and professional people, many of them influential in matters of national security. The sitting Air Force chief, Gen. David Jones, had taken a personal interest in the posting. Our first nominee failed the council's sniff check, and Jones was said to be embarrassed. An academic year at the council counted as senior professional education, and I'd already filled that square at National War College. Nonetheless, I was available and at loose ends. Would I be willing to go to New York and interview for the position, maybe rescue the Air Force's reputation? I would be and did, though at this point the council was also somewhat embarrassed for having refused our first candidate. I could have been fairly stale stuff and still skated through the interview.

In all, I got three months of French training. Afterward, I tried to continue learning the language on my own. For some years, I limited recreational reading to French, running through the Maigret series. There are more than seventy of these police procedurals, a bottomless resource if you give it the few minutes between going to bed and going to sleep. Georges Simenon puts down plain, unadorned French, clear enough to be read by anyone who can figure out traffic signals. Simenon is very special in this regard, but French itself seems inherently cleaner, more precise, a language of partitions. One of our blessings (or curses) is that English is so rubbery. We don't always do it, but we have at least the language for putting together a compromise.

I reported to the Council on Foreign Relations in the fall of 1975. My duties as Military Fellow carried no official content. It was entirely a self-starting proposition. I attended lectures as well as lunches and dinners at which I met various high-powered personalities. Bayless Manning headed the council, a distant figure with whom I had almost no contact. I made a lifelong friend of Zygmunt Nagorski, then in charge of membership programs. A man of considerable charm, Ziggy came in for some kidding on account of having been an officer in the Polish cavalry, an outfit with, at best, a spotty record. But no one could doubt his courage. One New York City evening, muggers attacked him and his wife, Marie. They must have seemed easy targets, both on the small side and well past middle age, but Zig put up a fight. He and Marie came away with possessions intact.

We lived at Fort Totten, an ancient coast-artillery post just outside the last subway stop at Flushing, Queens. The house, one of those old, drafty monsters built by the Army after the Spanish-American War, had high ceilings decorated in ornamental lead. A nice place, but not well maintained over the years, the plumbing and wiring desperate for attention. The post itself was beautifully situated and allowed for long walks around the battlements. Usually I drove to Shea Stadium, parked there and caught the train. A couple of transfers and half an hour later I was at the council's offices on Manhattan's Upper East Side. Riding the New York subway reminded me a little of survival school.

The council had no fitness facility, so I talked the National Guard into giving me a key to the Seventh Regiment Armory, on Park Avenue at 67th. There, I met regularly with a short list of local squash players who, like me, were not overstressed during normal duty hours.

The three service departments vied for two slots then set aside for Military Fellows resident at the council. During my time there, I shared office space with Army colonel Arthur "Gene" Dewey, who capped a fine military career by distinguishing himself as an administrator of international relief programs, becoming an assistant secretary of state in the Bush-43 administration.

The cover of *Time* magazine's September 8, 1975, issue featured the face of Air Force sergeant Leonard Matlovich, with the words, "I Am a Homosexual." A decorated Vietnam veteran and Roman Catholic convert to Mormonism who had voted for Goldwater in 1964, Matlovich was subsequently discharged from the Air Force, and he moved to California. He died of AIDS in 1988, age 44.

New York City was experiencing a financial crisis. Felix Rohatyn, an investment banker and member of the Council on Foreign Relations, resolved it by restructuring the city's debt.

In November 1975, Spain's General Francisco Franco died.

In January 1976, I returned to Nellis to play a part in rebuilding the dual-solo routine the Thunderbirds had abandoned after Mike Miller's accident with Jack Thurman. The team had been flying five-ship, single-solo shows for seven seasons but was set to return to a six-ship format in honor of the country's bicentennial. Since I was the most recent experienced lead solo, I was asked to help. I expected to fly a few sorties in the backseat with both Five and Six and was not looking forward to it since it's no fun being a passenger for this kind of work. But I figured I'd be out of there in a week.

The incumbent Number Five, Jim Simons, was a talented pilot and take-charge guy who had a year of single-solo experience under his belt. He had talked at length to the Blue Angel Solos and knew exactly what he wanted to do. When I offered some oral history—observations and lessons learned over the years—he paid zero attention. Lacy Veach, the new Number Six, was a good guy who had been a Misty with me in Vietnam. I tried to convince Simons his main job was to keep Veach alive, making no headway. Simons knew how to fly solo maneuvers. His approach: he would fly splendid, show-altitude figures, and Lacy would match them. Naturally (I explained), in due course Veach would be able to do just that, but at the start, the idea should be to fly maneuvers Lacy could mirror, then gradually work down to show altitude.

I briefed before our first training flight and climbed into Veach's backseat. The ride scared me. Simons did nothing the way I'd recommended. Following the mission, my suggestions during debrief made no impression. We flew a second sortie, a repeat of the first. I was writing the script, but Simons was making a different movie.

I never got to ride in Simons's backseat. After the two rides with Veach, I went to Chris Patterakis, my old buddy from the '67 team who was back as Thunderbird lead, and told him I was returning to the safety of New York City. I'd take my chances in the subway.

Somehow, Lacy Veach survived the year and went on to be a better Number Five. But he was turned off by the experience, eventually leaving the active Air Force and joining the Texas Air National Guard. He became an astronaut and got two rides in the space shuttle before cancer shortened his career and life.

When Simons left the team, he asked for a Navy exchange tour. A stickler for realism, he insisted on using actual combat, rather than training, switch settings. Doing otherwise, he said, reinforced negative learning. While flying with the Sixth Fleet, Simons managed to get off a live Sidewinder shot, dumping his wingman into the Med, an act not calculated to make the Navy happy. Surprisingly, it wasn't going to improve his career prospects in the Air Force, either. He, too, left the service, and last I heard, was flying for the airlines.

Every aircraft accident comes at the end of a sequence of events, each event reducing somewhat the available options. This is another way of saying that safe flying imposes a demand to retain as many options as practical. A pilot who refuses to use training settings in simulated combat willingly gives up an option, telling us all we need to know about his judgment.

With little else to do at the council, I sat down to write about Israel's security situation. It was my unspoken hope that *Foreign Affairs*, the council's justly celebrated quarterly, would accept an

My Armed Forces Staff College seminar.

With Joe Alon, in his Chevy Chase, Maryland, home, 1972.

*Three Thunderbird pilots at the National War College,
Class of 1974: center, Tom Swalm (later, Maj. Gen.);
right, Sam Johnson (later, Texas congressman).*

*National War College 1974 racquetball team, winners
of the Admiral Thomas H. Moorer Trophy.*

With Anwar Sadat, spring 1974.

With King Faisal of Saudi Arabia.

Flying the F-4, MacDill AFB, Florida, 1974.

article for publication, but the odds were not good. Few serving officers of any branch had ever published in this prestigious journal.

My proposed article argued that Israel's security did not require the retention of territories taken in 1967, but only that the real estate be demilitarized after being handed back. John Campbell, an eminent Middle East authority in residence at the council, read a draft and with great kindness recommended publication. Bill Bundy, the journal's editor, was also helpful, though we disagreed at first about how my name should appear at the top of the piece. Very few of my fighter pilot buddies would be regular readers of *Foreign Affairs*, but I wanted those who did come across the article to know it was me, so I told Bundy it had to be Colonel Merrill A. McPeak. He said the journal never used titles. They'd recently published an item by Queen Elizabeth II and had left out the Queen. I said, "OK, label me Merrill the First." A nice man, Bundy allowed the exception. "Israel: Borders and Security" appeared in the April 1976 number.[6]

The article caused no ripples I could detect in the United States, but there was a bit of a stir in Israel. The *Jerusalem Post* said the piece was probably not the work of some obscure Air Force colonel, but rather a State Department trial balloon sent aloft to test reaction in Tel Aviv.

Although aging—approaching 40 years old as this is written—sections of "Israel: Borders and Security" read well enough, even today. Of course, Israel held on to the Golan Heights, the Gaza Strip, East Jerusalem and the West Bank, a choice that more-or-less guaranteed its continued insecurity.

---

6 In those years, *Foreign Affairs* paid authors $500 for published articles. I asked for an opinion, and the Air Force's general counsel ruled I "could not accept compensation of any kind in addition to . . . Air Force pay and allowances." He was gracious, however, in wishing me "continued success in my literary efforts." I turned the check over to the Air Force Aid Society.

As the summer of 1976 approached, I had to leave the Council on Foreign Relations and return to the Air Force. My caretakers at Colonel Assignments came up with only two possibilities. Both were combat support group commander positions—one at Nellis, the other at RAF Mildenhall, in the UK. This was a great disappointment, since these were nonflying jobs and I had by now been out of the cockpit six and a half years, except for the brief period at MacDill. Besides, being in charge of base support had never been identified as a clear path to the top of the Air Force. Between the two positions in prospect, Nellis had far more scope, but it was in Tactical Air Command, an organization that had just cut me loose after less than six months at MacDill, and I wanted nothing further to do with it. So I opted to take the lesser job, arriving at Mildenhall in the middle of what for England was a severe drought. On descent for landing, the countryside looked about as brown as I'd ever seen it.

Chapter 5

Mildenhall

There's a lot of things they didn't tell me when I joined this outfit.

—Unknown Cowboy

Northwest Suffolk is low-lying country, forest and heath edged by Fenland. Here, human beings have scratched out a living since at least Mesolithic times. Roman engineers cleared some of the forest for roads, the countryside by then dotted with fortified farms. In the fourth century, worried about Saxon raids during a time of imperial instability, the Romans buried valuables like the Mildenhall Treasure, silver tableware unearthed in 1942 by a local plowman and now deposited in the British Museum. The Domesday Book carries an entry for Mildenhall, so we know that by 1086, 64 families lived here, and that they had a church and a mill. The fens were drained by the end of the nineteenth century, creating some of the most productive farmland in England. Even so, much of the ground is of marginal value, one reason why in the 1930s Royal Air Force chose the place as a site for one of its new-style bomber bases. There are many points of cultural interest to be seen within a few miles, including the town of Bury St. Edmunds and Cambridge University.

Glad to be back in the Air Force, even if not in a flying job, I threw myself into unfamiliar responsibilities. For one thing, there was lawn watering. My new duties included supervision of the civil engineers who maintained the base, including its buildings, roads, and grounds. British authorities had suspended lawn watering owing to the lack of rainfall, but Mildenhall had its own deep wells that were not much affected by the drought. We could have kept up appearances but had elected to share the pain with our neighbors rather than be the only green spot in East Anglia. My new boss, Col. Bill Thomas, the wing commander at Mildenhall, didn't much like the way the base looked and asked me to fix it. I spent considerable time face-to-face with water and sewage systems, never figuring out how to irrigate without offending the Brits. Mercifully, rain came before my lack of imagination could be fully exposed.

Without doubt, Bill Thomas was the best wing commander I ever worked for. He had snow-white hair and wore a neat mustache, which didn't matter because he was never going to make general anyway. His ah-shucks, country-boy routine couldn't hide the light-bulb always on behind the eyes. Starting as an enlisted man, he'd become a pilot via the aviation-cadet route and had flown tankers for many years. He had subsequently cross-trained into aircraft maintenance and been a very successful dirty-fingernails guy for outfits flying both large and small airplanes. In fact, he had come to Mildenhall from Torrejon, Spain, where he'd served as deputy commander for maintenance at the 401st Fighter Wing. This background made Bill Thomas a perfect fit for RAF Mildenhall.

Thomas's command was called the 513th Tactical Airlift Wing. It had only four aircraft permanently assigned to it, all modified KC-135s that functioned as flying command posts for SACEUR, the Alliance's senior commander. One of these was kept on alert at all times, ready to launch and provide NATO a survivable nuclear-release authority. From time to time, SAC reconnaissance aircraft dropped in. We supported the U-2, the SR-71, and a variety of highly modified C-135s doing electronic and other forms of surveillance. But the base's main purpose was to hold transport and tanker squadrons that came over on temporary assignment. C-130s from Military Airlift Command and KC-135s from Strategic Air Command rotated in from stateside to service in-theater requirements. Usually the crews stayed four to six weeks, living in dormitories, but they were on the road a good bit, carrying cargo or doing aerial refueling all across Europe. The transport and tanker capabilities were needed and probably should have been bedded down permanently and made part of the in-theater major command, United States Air Forces in Europe, or USAFE. Instead, crews and airplanes rotated in and out, and, to reduce cost, the Air Force had put the infrastructure in place to support successive rotations, these facilities belonging to the 513th Wing.

I suppose the TDY presence of MAC's C-130 squadron made the 513th a "tactical airlift" wing, but we might as easily have called ourselves a "tanker," a "reconnaissance," or some other kind of wing. I got the impression that not much thought went into how we named organizations. In any case, the basic job was support, and Bill Thomas had a deep understanding of every aspect of it, including what I was supposed to be doing with the combat support group.

With almost no aircraft of its own, the 513th was on the small side as wings go. Still, it incorporated virtually all the functions of a normal wing. In the mid-'70s, this meant the wing was organized around four major activities, each headed by a colonel. A deputy for operations (DO) supervised the flying squadrons, or would in a standard wing. This was the fighting part, the teeth of a wing, and most future wing commanders and generals came up through the DO side of the house. At Mildenhall, the DO had mostly an oversight function, babysitting the tanker and transport squadrons coming in on rotation.

A deputy for maintenance (DM) oversaw the first- and second-echelon of aircraft maintenance. The first echelon was at the flight line, where crew chiefs met and turned aircraft around, preparing them for subsequent flight. A good crew chief can fix just about anything, but a broken part he couldn't handle was often removed from the aircraft and sent to the second echelon, a bazaar of behind-the-line shops that specialized in hydraulic, electrical, engine, avionics, or other repair. (At a third echelon, depot maintenance, Air Force Logistics Command performed heavy work that could not be done economically at home station. When the depot couldn't fix it, we sent the pieces back to the manufacturer, the final, or fourth echelon of maintenance.)

The large, enlisted-heavy DM organization created a different sort of leadership problem for its senior officers. Many of the officers in DM leadership slots were ex-aircrew—older pilots and especially navigators—who had to find a way to add value doing something other than operations if they wished to remain in the Air Force. In a field as difficult and demanding as aircraft maintenance, some did not make a successful career transition.

A deputy for resource management (RM) supervised the activities of the supply squadron, transportation squadron, and the accounting and finance section. Supply handled receipt, inventory, storage, and issue of fuel, munitions, supplies, and equipment. These duties required a large squadron and sizeable storage facilities. Transportation, which included both operations and upkeep of ground vehicles, was more than just a motor pool, the straightforward job of keeping staff cars and buses in running order. Many different kinds of specialized vehicles—forklifts, munitions loaders, exotic cargo-handling equipment—had to be cared for. As for accounting and finance, in the old days, they kept a lot of cash on hand, so commanders could line up the men at the end of the month and pay them in person, a transaction thought to inspire loyalty. But by the mid-'70s, payday had lost its personal touch, and accounting and finance's most important duty was keeping track of the wing's outlays in the execution year and preparing next year's budget. Probably the least important of the wing's senior positions, the RM was likely a topped-out colonel who should be preparing for Civvy Street.

All of these officers—the DO, DM, and RM—were deputies, not commanders. They supervised squadron commanders, who reported through them to the wing commander, but none of them had the legal authority normally resident in a commander, such as the power to administer discipline or convene courts-martial.

I was the combat support group commander, last in the senior-officer lineup. The idea was, when war came, the wing packed up and went to the fight, taking with it what it could, but abandoning the base and anything that couldn't be moved. Someone had to be in charge of what was left behind, a duty falling to the support group commander, who for this reason was also called the base commander. This was my job at Mildenhall. It included the expected functions. The base had to be secured: I had a security police squadron. Its roads, grounds, and buildings must be maintained: I had a civil engineer squadron. I also had responsibility for many miscellaneous support functions not large enough to justify a squadron. Temporary housing (billeting), dining halls, the club system, a gymnasium, athletic fields, and other recreational facilities were organized as part of the morale, welfare, and recreation division. A personnel division offered education programs, career counseling, and support for assignment and promotion actions. A modest administration branch provided publication, duplication, and distribution service. And so forth.

Thus, even a small base like Mildenhall had plenty of colonel-level supervision. The wing commander was the boss. Both he and his vice-commander were colonels. The four major subordinates—the DO, DM, RM, and base commander—were colonels, and some of their deputies might also be colonels, as I had been when serving as assistant DO of the 1st Wing at MacDill. The wing commander certainly ought to be able to run the operation with all this senior talent on hand. But, in addition, some important functions were not under local control because they were not part of the wing's structure. For instance, a detachment of Air Force Communications Command handled the base's air traffic, manning the control tower and maintaining local radio aids. A detachment of the Air Weather Service did observation and forecasting. Few activities are more important to the DO than air traffic control or weather forecasting, but he did not directly supervise these functions. The base exchange (a sort of department store) and the commissary (a grocery store) provided needed services to the base's population, but they were detachments of the Army and Air Force Exchange Service and the Air Force Commissary Service, respectively. I cooperated with the local commanders, and they were likely to return my phone calls, but they did not work for me, a small irritant.

Another minor annoyance: two job titles—wing commander and base commander. Nobody in the wing or on the base had any doubt about who was boss, but we had an active program of outreach to the local community, and British civilians did have a problem with the nomenclature. The RAF counterpart of our wing commander was called a station commander, which was easy to confuse with base commander. Usually, the station commander was a group captain (colonel equivalent) in charge of all the activities at an RAF base, including flying operations. Moreover, an RAF station commander would likely have many officers with the rank of wing commander (lieutenant colonel equivalent) working for him. Thus, our arrangement, in which the base commander worked for the wing commander, puzzled our local Brit supporters. They charged it to colonial ineptitude.

It was from the brand new RAF Station Mildenhall that planes took off in 1934 for the Great Air Race—England to Melbourne, Australia. C. W. A. Scott and Tom Campbell Black won the race in a DH 88 Comet, covering the distance in an extraordinary 71 hours. Roscoe Turner and Clyde Pangborn finished third flying a Boeing 247D, now in the Smithsonian. Jackie Cochran withdrew after a hard landing at Bucharest damaged her aircraft.

There being more than enough colonels on base, we were assigned a rather small set of government quarters—so slight, indeed, that we opted out of the annual Holiday Parade through Homes, a local tradition. Ellie thought about doing more on her economics doctorate at Cambridge, but by now my moving her around from place to place had made this pretty tough, and, anyway, she was rather busy with the ex-officio duties issued to wives of senior military officers. She took her turn at the thrift shop, an institution performing worthy service, since enlisted families were anything but overpaid. She was an adviser to the NCO Wives Club, a particularly sensitive assignment, as wives sometimes bristle at the officer-enlisted divide. At Mildenhall, this club was under orders to produce a constitution, a task virtually guaranteed to generate heat, and Ellie somehow managed to pull the effort out of the flames. She was the best I'd ever seen at handling this kind of thing. Her general intelligence gave her stand-alone prestige, she didn't take herself too seriously, and she never traded on my rank or position.

I had much to learn about running an air base. In particular, I spent a lot of time with the civil engineers. As an enlisted man, Bill Thomas had worked in a civil engineer squadron, so he knew how the business operated, and I couldn't stand to be measurably dumber than he was. In addition, if we could save any money in executing the wing's budget, Thomas had a reasonable amount of discretion to fund modification and upgrade of our facilities, a special passion of his. I needed to have lots of renovation projects designed and ready to be let for bids, especially near the end of the fiscal year, when there was a sort of Klondike, a rush to obligate funds before they expired. This event—Thomas called it Operation Eagle Unclutch—occurred within a few weeks of my arrival at Mildenhall.

As an added complication, my civil engineer squadron had only a handful of uniformed Air Force personnel. Most of the management and all the work was done by British civilians on the payroll of the Property Services Agency (PSA), a classic bureaucracy charged, in this case, with the care and feeding of British public property. It was a special diplomacy challenge to get local PSA supervision to pay any attention to my agenda, and harder still to get productivity from the rank and file during a 36-hour week. PSA's maintenance personnel specialized in something we impertinent Yanks called the Look and Leave Team. Responding to emergency repair calls—many in the bathroom category, the Brits still having fits with plumbing—they usually sent two competent-looking people, a journeyman and an apprentice, who gave the problem a quick once-over and went back to the office, leaving the baffled customer to wait for real repairmen.

My security police squadron was all American but presented another sort of test. The squadron was divided into two sections. One flight, responsible for law enforcement, stationed people at the front gate to wave through properly registered vehicles. This flight also responded to crimes and had a small investigative section. Law enforcement can be a busy place. Like any small city police department, we had desk sergeants who chronicled the events of each 24 hours. Every morning, just as I got to work, the police brought me this blotter. I found it a bad way to start the day. Most blotter entries logged police rounds or substantiated routine checks, but the exceptions, and the goings-on they highlighted, were never good news.

The other, much larger security police flight had the job of defending the base. The size of this organization was dictated by the large number of posts strung along the perimeter fence and the need to man these positions around the clock during increased threat conditions. Day to day, these guys didn't have much to do, so they tended to get in trouble—ironically, my worst discipline problem. More than once, local police rang me up, asking whether I could come bail one or more of these policemen out of jail. Eventually, the locals gave me a badge, making me an honorary member of the Suffolk Constabulary.

All together, about 1,000 people worked for me in the combat support group.

This was our second tour in the UK, at our third station in the country. Things had changed a bit. Restaurant cooking had improved some in the decade since we were last assigned here. (OK, it was still not Italy.) They'd switched to decimal currency, a big shame, as Ellie had attained complete mastery of the ha'penny, shilling, and guinea. Harold Wilson was prime minister, ruling with a razor-thin margin and destined to be displaced in a couple of years by Maggie Thatcher.

Mao Zedong died in September 1976. Almost immediately the Cultural Revolution was abandoned, beginning a major policy turnaround.

In November, Jimmy Carter took the White House away from Gerald Ford.

Soon after my arrival, we staged the Mildenhall Air Fête, one of the largest air shows in Europe. It was a complex undertaking. Aircraft from around NATO flew in for static display. There were numerous flying demonstrations, the RAF's Red Arrows providing a finale. The Brits love an air show, and huge crowds converged on the base for the two-day affair, providing customers for shops and stalls set up along the flight line. We cleared out a large hangar to make room for a sort of flea market, renting space to peddlers from all over the UK and taking a cut of the revenue. Volunteers from the base's off-duty activities—Boy Scouts, thrift shops, clubs, sports teams, church groups—manned food and beverage booths. The income generated by the Air Fête would fund these activities for the next year.

Everybody had a great time, except me. I got to tackle the parking, security, and cleanup problems, which were substantial. By way of compensation, I retained the T-shirt concession for my outfit, the combat support group. I drew up a design with stylized Red Arrows pulling up into a loop and found enough money to make the down payment on a very large order, taking some risk. If the weather turned bad, I'd be stuck with a big bill to pay and enough unsold T-shirts to outfit the Group of Soviet Forces Germany. But the weather cooperated, and the T-shirt was a blockbuster best seller, swelling our base non-appropriated fund to record size.

I had a female staff sergeant in my office, a sort of adviser on women's issues. One day she ran in, obviously distressed. Someone had discovered the body of one of our enlisted women, drowned in a bathtub in the women's dormitory. I headed over there, cordoned off the place, started an inquiry.

We uncovered a lot during the investigation of what turned out to be a suicide. The young woman had been trying to get our attention, using everything but semaphore. She was on the weight-control program, had been involved in a number of alcohol-related incidents, had lost her job and was handing out towels at the gymnasium for something to do while we out-processed her. It was almost as though she'd been carrying around a sign saying, "I'm about to do something really stupid," and either we didn't notice or didn't care.

Various parts of the organization had all the information needed, but we didn't put it together and therefore lost the young lady. Lesson learned.

The club complex—separate social clubs for enlisted, NCOs, and officers—was one of my biggest management headaches. Rather, the Officers Club was a problem, the other two doing quite nicely. Since Bill Thomas went to the Officers Club regularly, any defect in the facility or service got me unwanted attention.

Thomas hated undoing those little packets butter came in. (In this respect, he was well ahead of the national anxiety about packaging, a modern bane.) Because he sometimes breakfasted at the club, I made sure we had some butter open and ready for him to spread. Whenever we got distinguished visitors, which was often, Thomas test-drove the VIP quarters, usually rediscovering the quaintness of English plumbing. Loo pull chains demanded an educated yank, but PSA engineers could do some fine-tuning if they were so inclined. Thomas ordered up such service often.

The Officers Club's main problem was more basic: solvency. Bill Thomas was on my case about the club's financial problems because he wanted to fix it up. For years, Congress had subsidized failing clubs but was no longer willing to use tax dollars for this purpose. Any renovation or remodeling would have to be funded from self-generated profit, of which there was none.

Frankly, the O. Club should have been profitable. If we regarded it as a business, there were essentially three revenue streams: members paid a small monthly fee into an administrative account; a restaurant sold food; a bar sold drinks. In the civilian world, both bars and restaurants make money, and they don't charge dues or enjoy cost advantages like no rent or free utilities. Moreover, if an Officers Club could work anywhere, it ought to be at a base like Mildenhall, with a large rotational population in and out on temporary duty. In fact, our NCO Club was very profitable, while the Officers Club regularly lost money in large denominations, principally because it couldn't attract patronage.

I hit on the idea of running an afternoon bus into the nearby town of King's Lynn, offering free rides back to the base. A considerable number of young Englishwomen took advantage of this service. Soon, our club was humming with all the business it could handle. We generated a profit and launched a program to upgrade the facility.

I worried a little about my business model because Bill Thomas's boss, the commander of Third Air Force, was Maj. Gen. (later

Lt. Gen.) Evan Rosencrans. I'd known Rosie in Vietnam, where he had been Bill Creech's assistant at Phu Cat. He was a marvelous officer, but nothing if not a straight arrow. With his headquarters at Mildenhall, he lived and worked close enough to notice the much-increased activity in the Officers Club. It was career suicide if he found out how I was making the club profitable.

As I neared the end of a year as base commander, General Rosencrans called me into his office to say I'd be going to Zaragoza, our training base in northern Spain, as wing vice-commander. This return to flying duty was in principle a step up from the combat support group. However, like Mildenhall, Zaragoza was not a "real" wing, with real combat aircraft and responsibilities. It was a training wing whose main asset was the gunnery range at Bardenas Reales. Rosencrans, who apparently had retained high regard for me—meaning either he had not learned of or had decided to ignore my strategy for healing Officers Club finances—told me he'd tried to get me a better job but this was the best he could manage.

We packed up and left Mildenhall, one year to the day after arriving there.

Chapter 6

Zaragoza

I have always felt the inutility and inconvenience of the office of second-in-command . . . Every officer in an army should have some duty to perform . . .
—Wellington, Letter to Marshal Beresford

Located in northern Spain's Ebro Valley, Zaragoza was the bed-down base of the 406th Tactical Fighter Training Wing. Aircraft from other European bases deployed to Zaragoza for gunnery training in much the same way we used to go to Libya in the '60s. The weather was pretty good, and the gunnery range at Bardenas Reales was better than anything in the UK or Germany. Continental squadrons came down to Zaragoza with little more than airplanes, pilots, and crew chiefs, so, like Mildenhall, the 406th Wing provided the full array of base support functions.

I got recurrent in the F-4 and flew some, but there was a strict limit on the amount we could fly, since we cadged time meant for pilots from the deploying wings. Not doing as much flying as I needed to, I continued to show signs of lost proficiency. One day at Bardenas, I got thrown off the range for pressing too low on practice dive-bomb attacks. The range officer worked for me back at Zaragoza, so this took some nerve. But I fouled two passes in a row, and he said, "Safe 'em up and go home," the right call on his part but embarrassing for me.

Some think that flying becomes automatic, like riding a bike or swimming, and that's true for recreational aspects of the craft. It's fighting in the air that must be polished like the family silver. Nobody, not even the world's greatest fighter pilot, can stop flying for long periods and expect to stay good at air combat.

Zaragoza air base had two long, parallel runways built by Strategic Air Command in the years when it pulled alert overseas with B-47s. By the 1970s, the Spanish Air Force had flying squadrons and support facilities on one side of the base, and we had buildings and infrastructure on the other, but it would be a mistake to speak of "our" side and "theirs." The Spanish made it clear it was their base—all of it.

The colonels supervising an Air Force wing all made the same salary, so the status differentiator was the set of government quarters assigned. Here at Zaragoza, Ellie and I had the second-best house, a very nice, Spanish-style hacienda, bleachy white, with a red-tile roof. Anything would grow in the surrounding garden, if you watered it. Spanish groundskeepers kept the broadleaf lawn under control and tended flowerbeds that held a variety of exotic, semitropical plants.

There was a cantina just outside the main gate, called the Shack. We went there about once a week. For a few pesetas, they served up a bowl of white-bean soup, a tossed salad with lots of fresh tomatoes, and some Spanish *pan* that reminded you why you didn't like Wonder Bread. Downtown, in an interesting set of alleyways known as the Tubes, we could get *rioja* and *tapas* late into the night. Life was good.

Legend had it Zaragoza played an important role in the

beginnings of Christianity in Spain. On religious holidays, supplicants still paraded through downtown, flagellating themselves with rods or switches that welted the back and made it bleed, the spectacle holding a certain morbid fascination, I suppose, but something I needed to see only once.

The Spanish Air Force did enlisted training on their side of the base, periodically inviting us to flag-kissing ceremonies. Nationalist in the extreme, these rituals had heavy religious overtones: for God and Spain. Still, it was touching to watch the column of raw, innocent youngsters file past to kiss the hem of their nation's colors. Some recruits had the empty look of rejects sent to "the army" on account of low potential. The SAF produced much of its own food, tilling land and grazing herds on its aerodromes. Here was an air force in which shepherd was still a perfectly good job title.

Being vice-commander was an awful job. The wing commander, Col. Harley Wills, was a solid pilot and quite competent, maybe a little disappointed he didn't have a "real" wing to command. Not only did we have no aircraft of our own, we were tenants on a Spanish base, removing big chunks of meaningful work for Wills, let alone the two of us.

Typically, a basket of lesser responsibilities migrated from the wing commander to the vice. I was, for example, the so-called inspector general for complaints. Anyone who thought he'd been wronged in any way could come see me, and I was obliged to open a file, investigate, remedy any injury. By Air Force regulation, this responsibility devolved on the vice-commander, since the commander might be the source of the injustice. At most bases, race discrimination was a feature of many complaints, but we didn't have much of that at Zaragoza. The base was a magnet for Spanish-speaking officers and airmen; we had a high Latino quotient and a very good racial climate. I also headed the wing exercise team, charged with designing and grading local exercises

at improving our response to various combat scenarios and peacetime emergencies—aircraft crashes, fires, terrorist incidents, and
so forth. I chaired the base environmental committee, responsible
for tracking and improving compliance with a variety of Air Force
initiatives meant to reduce and remediate industrial pollution. I
paid attention to these duties and learned something of value from
each of them, but it was not the same as having actual responsibility for the organization's performance.

I looked around for something to do, giving special attention to
the parts of a wing where I had no hands-on experience. Here at
Zaragoza, we had a complete set of second-echelon maintenance
shops, doing off-aircraft work on engines, electrical, hydraulic, or
fuel systems, and supporting a variety of specialized tasks, like
canopy, ejection-seat, or drag-chute repair; pylon and gun maintenance; or fuel-tank servicing. I hung around these shops, learning something of their practices and procedures. Who took broken
parts off the airplane? Who decided whether to make repairs on station or send the part back to the depot for more specialized repair?
What happened to the repaired part? Who paid for what? Reams
of regulations provided complicated answers. The supply squadron
had rather substantial responsibilities, ordering everything from
boots, pencils, and gardening tools to the more exotic and valuable
aircraft spare parts. We had several large warehouses; keeping
track of inventory was a tough job. Again, I spent many hours in
storerooms, becoming familiar with the procedures that allowed us
to account for receipt, storage, and issue of thousands of line items
of supply.

I improvised a jogging route that gave me daily exposure to the
weather. The wind blew across Catalonia and through Aragon in
all seasons. In winter, fog piled up in the Ebro Valley, and it got
surprisingly cold.

Brian attended the base high school. Mark was now at MIT,
studying engineering.

Zaragoza had an annual People's Fest. Anybody in the wing could call our radio station and, in return for a charitable pledge, ransom a task and name a person who must do it. I was tagged to appear on the front steps of the base exchange, play the guitar and sing Johnny Paycheck's "Take This Job and Shove It."

At overseas bases, the host-tenant relationship is a variable having both a strategic and a tactical component. In 1977, the strategic relationship with Spain was fraying at the edges. American forces had been around for what seemed to the Spanish like a long time. We'd stayed here under terms hammered out in base-rights negotiations, an irritant always either under way or about to start up again. The negotiations themselves, let alone the terms they produced, were increasingly odious. It was important to the Spanish that their flag fly over the base; we displayed ours only indoors. Here in Spain, we were cut flowers—decorative, perhaps, but expected neither to grow nor spread.

Locally, the Spanish commander, a certain Colonel Timon, considered himself in charge of all base activities, tolerating us only so long as we behaved. Timon had come to his elevated station by virtue of service as cannon fodder in Franco's army during the civil war. He was by now an antique colonel, a pilot who didn't fly, a nice dresser, a stickler for form over substance. Naturally, he and Harley Wills couldn't stand each another, tact not being Wills's strong suit. The separation of our operation from theirs kept Timon and Wills physically apart, the only thing preventing complete collapse of the relationship.

As the designated envoy to Timon, I did my best. After all, we were guests in his country. In any case, I had to field his complaints. Wills wouldn't talk to him.

The first of a wave of serious films about the Vietnam War appeared in 1978, including Michael Cimino's *The Deer Hunter*. Jane Fonda won an Oscar for her work in the antiwar *Coming*

Home. Francis Ford Coppola's great *Apocalypse Now* debuted in 1979.

It was an awful job, except when the boss was gone. With Harley Wills off station, I was in charge of the place, and I reveled in it. It was not that I renamed the streets, but a completely different feeling goes with owning the ranch.

One weekend in early summer, Wills away on leave, a civil cargo transport aborted takeoff on our side of the base. The aircraft, an ancient Boeing 707, was en route from the UK to Saudi Arabia, maxed out by a heavy load of fertilized chicken eggs. The pilot had stopped for fuel on a Sunday because Zaragoza's runways were 13,000 feet long and he'd been concerned about aircraft weight. With summer temperatures stretching takeoff rolls, he wanted some concrete. His worry was justified: on takeoff, he was not fast enough at the refusal point and elected to abort. He locked up the brakes, blowing the tires, but finally got it stopped on the runway. I was called at home and hurried down to the flight line in shorts and flip-flops. One thing we did not want was a closed runway, even on a Sunday.

We couldn't tow the airplane until we jacked it up and put on new wheels. Our crews were well prepared to handle fighter-sized problems, but big airplanes were a little out of our league. We'd have to reduce aircraft weight before we could lift the thing with our equipment. We had formed a human chain and started unloading egg crates when Colonel Timon showed up in full dress uniform, this being Sunday, go-to-church day. I was in the middle of the fight, wrestling boxes out of the aircraft and sweating hard. Timon tried to act natural, but this was not the sort of appearance and behavior he expected of a senior officer, even making allowances for my being American. He spoke no English and my fighter pilot Spanish was limited to basics, but I was made to understand he wanted the aircraft removed from the runway. Following this constructive input, he departed.

It took us a while, but eventually we complied.

Timon was later promoted to brigadier general and retired to the sun and quiet of the Canary Islands, having lived a full life by most reckonings.

There were not many fat Spanish, a spare people in a spare land. They were proud, and pride makes for a powerful diet. In the evening, families put on good clothes, the children as fussed over as Velázquez's *Meninas*. Their walks together were measured, solemn. They passed neighbors with an air of neutrality, chose a sidewalk cafe, eyed tables, drew up chairs. They might drink a little wine but would treat public drunkenness or any form of personal excess with contempt. They were separate, proud inside their houses, trash tossed without intended insult into the commons, proud inside their frontiers, not much liking what they saw abroad. Among the nations of Europe, Spain sent out the fewest tourists.

Still, Franco had been dead for three years, and the country was making a careful, negotiated transition to representative democracy. While we watched, fascinated, they found the courage to adopt a new constitution and start the long join up with Europe.

A few weeks after the great chicken-egg incident, I was flying a low-level training sortie when the wing command post radioed a recall. Our major command, United States Air Forces in Europe, had asked that I report to the headquarters at Ramstein, Germany, for a job interview—quickly. Someone had fallen from grace, and they needed a replacement. I landed, went home for my shaving kit while the ground crew refueled the airplane, then flew up to Ramstein. USAFE's four-star commander also served as commander of Allied Air Forces Central Europe (AAFCE), with both headquarters collocated at Ramstein. It turned out the interview was at AAFCE headquarters. A British air vice-marshal, AAFCE's deputy for plans and operations, saw me. I was hired and told to report for work immediately.

I flew back to Zaragoza and packed up the furniture. The wing quickly laid on a going-away party. Colonel Timon showed up, a gesture that meant something since he'd never before attended any of our farewell dinners.

We left, one year to the day after arriving in Spain.

Logbook: Zaragoza, 1977–78

F-4D/E	88.7

Chapter 7

The Bunker

To find a form that accommodates the mess, that is the job of the artist now.

—Attributed to Samuel Beckett

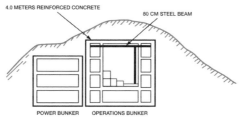

In the late 1970s, US forces stationed in Europe were controlled through two chains of command. For administration—the management of personnel, equipment, installations—US European Command (EUCOM) "owned" all American forces of any service. United States Air Forces in Europe (USAFE) served as the Air Force component of EUCOM. This national chain of command gave the United States a "go it alone" option in Europe, should the Alliance fail for any reason.

On the other hand, in Europe, the armed forces of the United States and its NATO allies were so tightly integrated it would have been nearly impossible to do any actual fighting except as part of the Alliance. In a crisis, EUCOM and its service components, including USAFE, moved under the NATO command structure, and the US national commander, CINCEUR (usually an Army four-star), put on his second hat as NATO's Supreme Allied Commander, Europe, or SACEUR.

Unhappily, the NATO chain of command was organized by geography, not service component. Thus, SACEUR had no air component reporting to him, but rather major subordinate commands for northern, central, and southern Europe. The USAFE commander's wartime job was to head the air force piece of Allied Forces Central Europe (AFCE), a very important post, but nevertheless a mismatch with his broader national responsibilities. In view of the importance of airpower in any defense of the Continent, we should have been concerned about assigning the Alliance's senior airman to a specific region, no matter how important, and effectively excluding him from strategic, theater-wide deliberations taking place at NATO's supreme headquarters. Airpower is by nature suited for ample horizons, for conflict-wide scope. Indeed, this is one of its principal assets, quickly depreciated when we give air forces a narrow, ground-centric focus. It's sort of the way the Army might organize for combat, if they still thought they'd gotten it right in Korea or Vietnam.

My new duties put me in the NATO chain of command for the Central Region. A British two-star, Air Vice-Marshal Ken Kingshot, was my immediate boss. He had offices at Ramstein, but my place of business was a large, underground facility located some kilometers northwest, in hills above the tiny village of Börfink— in the Hunsrück, after the Black Forest, the largest woods in the Federal Republic. Here, NATO had cleared off some trees, gouged a deep hole, dropped in a square, four-story concrete building, and pushed a lot of rock and dirt back over the top. The structure's roof was reinforced to withstand conventional bombing, and the whole place could be sealed up to operate at least for a while in a chemical or biological environment. It was a war headquarters, thinly manned except for exercises or the real thing.

According to our concept, on warning, the Central Region's overall commander, a German Army four-star located at Brunssum, in the Netherlands, and the US Air Force four-star at Ramstein would leave their above-ground, peacetime headquarters and report to the Börfink Bunker, bringing a large chunk of their staffs with them. The Bunker's skeleton manning would swell to over 300 people per 12-hour shift, as it became the joint wartime headquarters directing the ground and air defense of Europe's vital Central Region. My main responsibility was to keep the Bunker "warm," that is, awake and ready to operate immediately upon the arrival of Alliance airmen who would take over direction of air combat operations in Central Europe.

Much money, perhaps a billion dollars, had gone into building and equipping the Börfink Bunker. NATO's annual infrastructure budget covered much of the cost, but it would have taken much too long to complete the project by relying on this funding source alone, so Germany and the United States had put in a good bit of national money. The Germans made a major investment in the physical plant; we bought and installed most of the command, control, communications, computer, and intelligence gear. After completing construction, we allowed the place to operate for a few months, a sort of shakedown cruise, then with some fanfare brought in the four-stars for their first major exercise, which turned out to be an embarrassing fiasco. Naturally, some of the phones connected to nothing, understandable and easily forgiven, considering the complicated nature of modern communications. Much the same could be said for the computer-generated, large-screen displays. We knew about their balkiness, and, anyway, the information they were supposed to show was not getting through to the Bunker. But doorknobs came loose in the hand, wall switches failed to illuminate, toilets refused to flush, jackets hung on pegs slid to the floor. Nothing—repeat, nothing— worked right. A US Air Force colonel, my immediate predecessor, got the sack on account of this, unfairly, near as I could tell. In any case, Air Vice-Marshal Kingshot told me with a straight face that I'd been brought in to make the Bunker *work as advertised* (emphasis his).

Börfink Bunker was a command and control facility, maybe the most advanced in the world outside the United States. But just what is "command and control?"[7] Armies have been doing something like it since the days of jungle drums, so we understand intuitively what's going on here. In essence, command and control is a system for directing attacks on targets. Artillerymen have a motto: "shoot, move, and communicate." But who to shoot at? Where to move to? How and with whom to communicate? A command and control apparatus, the brains of combat, must answer these questions, and since commanders believe the side with the most evolved central nervous system will dominate, they have great incentive to find and use the leverage associated with advances in command and control.

However, modern command and control is quite complex, involving the integration of many disparate systems and disciplines, each in itself a job to master. It's the sort of thing that in later years would be called a system of systems. (Whenever you hear such a term, you can be quite confident the resulting structure will carry only a modest load.) We had no school that taught the subject, no exactly congruent Air Force occupational specialty. Without thinking much about it, we assumed that if officers from the various related disciplines—operations, intelligence, communications, weather, security, civil engineering, computer support—gathered in a room, command and control would happen, just as enough monkeys and typewriters will eventually produce *Richard III*.

By this point in my career, I'd spent a lot of time observing the goings-on in various command centers and had some idea how the

---

7 We used to speak, simply, of command and control, or "C2," but over the years the terminology has been unstable, a warning of trouble. The nomenclature morphed through several stages: C3, C3I, C4. At this writing, "C4ISR" is the term *du jour*. For this volume, I return to the usage "command and control" because I believe the other two Cs— computers and communications—are gadgets, and that intelligence, surveillance, and reconnaissance are operations support functions.

business worked, at least the basics. But Börfink Bunker was in a different class altogether from the local command posts I'd inhabited and, truthfully, I had many questions about the larger, conceptual issues of command and control. The science writer and editor James Gleick observed that scientists have a tough-guy vocabulary for describing difficult problems. A thing is said to be *obvious* if an expert practitioner can understand it after years of study. *Not obvious* means the discoverer should be nominated without delay for a Nobel Prize. For the most opaque physical problems, ones that require a genuine leap of imagination, scientists reserve the word *deep*. I came to regard command and control as a deep problem. It's not so much physics as metaphysics.

I had to figure out "What is it?" and also, since the Bunker needed to *start working*, "How do you do it?"—or maybe "Where can I get some?" At the beginning, I felt fortunate in one thing: Börfink was such an important, new facility, experts from all over the world paraded by for a look-see. I was eager for such visits, thinking I might get a few tips, and chagrined when none of the "experts" gave me a straight answer. Instead, they ended up asking me questions.

At warfare's molecular level, command and control is the carbon that makes covalent bonding of combat units possible. Still unsure of the chemistry, I was supposed to get the mixture right.

This was our first assignment in the Federal Republic, though I'd flown in and out of the place many times over the years. We moved into an apartment the Army owned in the village of Birkenfeld. Two bedrooms, one bath. Now more than 40 years old and a full colonel for years, I felt slightly mistreated, especially the business about one bathroom. But with Mark away at university there were only three of us, and we made do. Our flat was in A Building, one of four Stalinist apartment blocks that comprised what the Army called the Birkenfeld Military Community. Because of my status as senior resident, the Army declared me "mayor" at this outpost.

The closest American military presence was the large Army base at Baumholder (our name: "Mudholder"). Here, in 1937, Hitler had expropriated 30,000 acres, cleared out 14 villages and created a large training ground on which his panzers could fire and maneuver. It was now a US installation, complete with post exchange, commissary, and dependent school. Brian and the other kids living in Birkenfeld bussed the 15 kilometers, including some dandy hairpin bends climbing up to the Baumholder Plateau. An Army two-star (a thoroughly nice man named Rick Brown) held court at Baumholder, standing me in a brace when there was any trouble at Birkenfeld. He was also the authority with whom I could register complaints on behalf of constituents of Buildings A through D.

Our buildings stood at the northern edge of Birkenfeld, a small place in a rural setting, only about 7,000 people living there. But the town had the enhanced standing of a district administrative center, or *Landkreis,* within the State of Rhineland-Palatinate. It also boasted a traffic signal, the only one in half-an-hour's drive and much used for orientation when giving directions. Naturally, German pedestrians waited for the light to change, even though vehicular traffic posed no danger. (They also dutifully obeyed a law requiring residents to clear snow from the sidewalk in front of their property by 9:00 a.m.) Near the traffic signal, Gasthaus zum Römer featured a good schnitzel, pommes frites, nourishing German beer, and if you were in luck, a seat at the *Stammtisch,* the table nominally reserved for regulars. On New Year's Eve, the town put up fireworks that bounced light off blankets of ice and snow, reflecting into a sky that was crystal clear and snappy cold.

All Germans study English in school, but the solid citizens of Birkenfeld quickly lost fluency owing to a lack of practice. Ellie picked up a workmanlike German for use when shopping for groceries.

Perhaps we should have felt a little isolated here, but we didn't.

In September, with help from Jimmy Carter, Anwar Sadat and Menachem Begin signed the Camp David Accords, under which

Israel returned the Sinai Desert to Egypt. The parties could have built on this development but, owing to shortsightedness on both sides (most notably Israel's continuing settlement of the occupied territories), it led only to "cold peace." Nevertheless, the balance of forces in the Middle East changed, at least for the moment, and maybe for a long time.

On Christmas Day, 1978, Vietnam invaded Cambodia to depose Pol Pot, head of one of history's most murderous regimes. Phnom Penh fell in January. Cambodia's ally, China, crossed Vietnam's northern border at the end of January, hoping to punish Hanoi for its victory. Chinese forces were beaten back, suffering a remarkable, humiliating defeat.

Following a year of escalating unrest, the Shah of Iran fled Tehran, and the Ayatollah Khomeini returned from exile.

In March, at Pennsylvania's Three Mile Island, the United States experienced its worst nuclear accident to date.

As assistant chief of staff (ACOS) for current operations, I was in charge of about 35 officers and men from the six contributing countries of the Central Region: the United States, United Kingdom, Germany, Netherlands, Belgium, and Canada. My deputy was Deiter Frese, a Luftwaffe lieutenant colonel and pilot. This small unit constituted the Central Region Air Operations Center (CRAOC). We manned our part of the Bunker, keeping it open 24 hours a day, seven days a week. To stay busy, we monitored the peacetime operations of Allied wings in the Central Region as they executed their daily flying schedules. (I supposed this explained the "current operations" part of my job title.) We also kept close track of Warsaw Pact air activity on the other side of the inner-German border. If the Pact could manage a surprise attack—pretty unlikely—then in theory I would assume tasking authority and run the air war, at least until a more senior AAFCE officer showed up at the Bunker.

I had a little extra clout because I was dual-hatted. That is, in addition to being ACOS, current ops, I also served as AAFCE's senior representative at the Bunker. A few people from other parts of the AAFCE staff were not part of the operations center, but did show up for work every day at the Bunker, and I was their on-scene supervisor. More important, especially with regard to intelligence, I was also USAFE's senior representative, with responsibility for the US national presence at the Bunker. One whole floor of the Bunker dealt with compartmented intelligence, requiring something more than normal security clearances, so only a few properly cleared US personnel could enter. In fact, I had more people working for me in this national role than served under me on the Allied side.

I was one of three full colonels who were major players at the Bunker. The Central Region's overall joint commander (the German four-star) also kept the Bunker warm with his senior representative (a German Army colonel) and perhaps 50 Allied officers and men. The Bunker itself, the real estate, belonged to the German Air Force, so there was a so-called Bunker commander, a Luftwaffe colonel, who had perhaps another 75 or so German Air Force personnel performing security and housekeeping duties. This arrangement made for another of those interesting problems in Alliance diplomacy since, for security reasons, neither of these two gentlemen had access to a large part of the facility they were supposed to own, a situation they resented a bit. Before my arrival, the colonel triumvirate had been engaged in a full-contact tug-of-war, the resulting standoff being one of the reasons nothing in the Bunker worked. Immediately, I proposed the three of us form a committee to establish procedures and referee the inevitable jurisdictional disputes. We did so and quickly forged relationships allowing us to work well in harness.

I also had to rebuild morale, which was scraping bottom in my little operation. By and large, airmen disliked working here, subterranean duty not something ordinarily held out as an inducement to potential air force recruits of any country. In addition, my crew had failed its first major test, they didn't know what to do about it, and they had their heads down. Therefore, I scheduled a Friday beer call. In good weather, I occasionally took everybody outside for a picnic. I designed and ordered up a unit plaque so that, after departure, people would have something to hang on their I-love-me wall. Slowly, we began to operate as a team. Even the Dutch guys started pretending they liked the Germans, though I didn't press them too hard on this.

Landkreis Birkenfeld encompassed an area of about 85 square miles, half of it forest, a third agriculture, the rest wasteland, constructed area, roads, and the Baumholder training ground. The district mapped almost perfectly to the upper catchment basin of the Nahe, a typical subalpine river of inconstant water level. Summer could pretty much dry it up, but the river made good its claim after heavy rain or snow thaw. Most of the Hunsrück's streams and brooks flowed into the Nahe, which itself emptied eventually into the Rhine, at Bingen. It would seem a little far north to grow grapes here, but the slate soil absorbed solar energy and the river's microclimate moderated temperatures, so the locals bottled some quite good white wine under the Nahe label.

Thus, forestry and agriculture gave the landscape its character. The whole district had fewer than 100,000 inhabitants, nearly half of them crowded into Idar-Oberstein, where for the past 150 years or so stonecutters had used local and imported materials to produce fine jewelry. I wasn't so high on the jewelry, thinking the town more rightly deserved to be famous for its *Spiessbraten,* a sort of a pork steak, treated and roasted over open fire.

Making NATO's leading-edge command and control facility work depended first on getting a contribution from the regular crew that manned the place in peacetime. Only a few lived in Birkenfeld. This would correct itself in time, but for now the Bunker was new, and (unlike us) European air forces didn't move their people around at the drop of a hat. So most of my crew lived at Ramstein, where they caught an eight o'clock bus and arrived at the Bunker midmorning, pretty close to the lunch break. By about three p.m., they were preparing to reembark. The workday was portal to portal, so, with skill and cunning, I could get a normal duty day of maybe four hours out of these guys.

Moreover, an informal competition existed inside the Alliance, a sort of arms race to see how many holidays member countries could declare and how much leave their people could take. All the nations were good at this, with Belgium the acknowledged titleholder. When the Belgian king decided citizens should get an additional day off after Christmas, the prime minister rose to the bait, countering with the day after New Year's. My Belgian officers and NCOs already were assured 45 days' annual leave, the clock not running until they crossed the Belgian frontier inbound. In addition, Belgian pilots went home regularly for proficiency flying. If lucky, I'd see a Belgian flying type maybe 100 days a year—for four hours a day.

The work environment wasn't much help, either. The Bunker's characterizing feature was an enormous theater—rows of desks facing stacked large-screen displays that in exercise or war would show the ground and air situation in the Central Region, the status of critical resources, the weather picture, and the like. In full cry, officers and NCOs planning military operations would pile into this room and bring it alive with movement and sound. Galleries of windowed offices rimmed the command center, workplaces for support staff. These, too, would become hyperactive when the chips were down. But in peacetime the place was an echo chamber—the theater vacated, the displays blank, the peripheral offices deserted. Our small, peacetime crew disappeared into this cavernous, industrial space, leaving almost no impression. It was the opposite of human scale, too big, unfixable. Down here, we were spelunking, maybe lost and, accordingly, under almost no social pressure to produce.

Meanwhile, the Bunker crew had difficult problems to solve. Take, for example, the matter of friendly-unit reporting. The information we had about the enemy, that is to say intelligence, was taken from him, mostly without his cooperation. It was not 100 percent reliable, and we knew this and made allowances. What we didn't grasp (or refused to admit) was that the intelligence picture we built up of the enemy might in fact be more accurate and insightful than the understanding we had of our own side, which was based on information we got through reporting systems that relied on cooperation.

To direct combat operations we needed to know the condition of subordinate units. (Are you there? Do you have airplanes? Are you out of ammunition? Is the runway open?) In addition, various staff elements inside the Bunker had to track the status of corresponding functions in order to provide support. Our medics wanted to know if the local base hospital was undamaged and how many tongue depressors were on hand. Our weather staff must understand if local observers and forecasters were still alive and well— and so forth. Thus, every function at every Allied air base in the Central Region sent lengthy reports to the Bunker on a regular schedule. Naturally, subordinate units saw such reporting as a loathsome workload, generally delegated to an enlisted conscript of questionable motivation who spoke little or no English.

My staff at the Bunker was in charge of writing the manual on how friendly units would do such status reporting. By the time we incorporated all the sample message forms and procedures for filling them out and encoding them, the manual approached the size of the Chicago phone book. People we expected to use this tome would never read and understand it. No load-shedding scheme existed. That is, as the lights went out in a deteriorating combat situation, we had no way to skinny down reporting so as to eliminate nice-to-have and still get minimum essential information. The whole rickety structure either stood or collapsed entirely, a formula for failure. The officer I had in charge of writing this manual was a Belgian major, a flying type.

Because I lived nearby and came to work early, I had a couple of hours before the morning bus from Ramstein showed up, quiet time during which I worked alone on problems, like the manual for friendly-unit status reporting. Gradually, I cleared away some of the underbrush.

It was 12 minutes by staff car from our apartment in Birkenfeld to the Bunker's entrance, by way of a country road that climbed north out of the village into the Hunsrück. This drive was in many ways the best part of the day. Built-up areas in the valley soon hid from view, so at first I saw only scattered farmhouses and the rolling hills that supported extensive agriculture. Here I made daily sightings of the European common buzzard, a magnificent creature so handsome it surely should protest the name. Then the countryside transitioned from field to *Hochwald* (high forest), ideal for hiking or other outdoor recreation, with many deer, rare plants, clear streams, the best air quality in the Federal Republic. Were I to continue north, the road would take me at right angles across the Hunsrückhöhenstrasse, the ancient Roman highway running from Trier to Mainz, and deposit me at length at Bernkastel, a lovely, medieval town on the Moselle. Instead, I turned off, heading west down a narrow lane leading toward Börfink, then turned again, short of the village, into the small, camouflaged cantonment that incorporated the Bunker. I parked near what looked like the entrance to a mine, though this one had huge, solid-looking blast doors, and made the long walk through a tunnel to an elevator that took me down into a netherworld of artificial light.

Judging whether we are ready for a fight is a problem as old as war, I suppose. By now, I'd spent much of a career addressing this matter for individual aircrews and for tactical squadrons and wings.

But rating the readiness of pilots and air units was by nature fairly straightforward (and didn't add much expense) because what they did day-to-day pretty well resembled what they might do in combat. Here at the Bunker, we needed to make a much more abstract judgment. We wanted to know whether we could in an instant rely on a command and control system essentially unused in peacetime to direct very large assemblies of air and ground units in high-intensity combat in the middle of Europe.

To make such a judgment, the Alliance staged several large exercises a year. To a first approximation, these exercises answered the question "Are we ready?" Equally important, they identified shortcomings and suggested remedies. (For instance, years of exercises exposed peacetime headquarters as obvious, stationary, quite soft targets, a deficiency that led eventually to building Börfink Bunker.) Thus, a significant part of each NATO headquarters staff devoted itself to planning and conducting exercises. With the commander's guidance, they figured out what to test and how to test it. It was not easy work.

Suppose the issue concerned whether enemy movements were noted and reported, and prompted an appropriate reaction. During an exercise, a trusted agent would hand a scrap of paper to, say, the lieutenant in charge of a cavalry platoon keeping a certain bridge under observation. The note might say, "Leading units of the Soviet Sixth Guards Tank Army are crossing the bridge, headed west." The first question: does this information ever get to higher authority? (Very often, it does not.) If it does, is the reporting accurate? (Usually it comes out garbled in exactly the same way that people at a party corrupt information whispered around a circle.) Does it arrive in time for headquarters to take effective action? (Count on the Sixth Guards Tank Army to be well clear of the bridge before we do anything about it.) And this would be one small data point in a closely scripted, three-day exercise that might feature thousands of such test inputs.

Exercise planning thus consumed much of the work year for each NATO headquarters. Lots of staff effort went into thinking about how to test the system, writing the inputs that fed into an exercise to make it interactive, and grading the result. Smaller scale, command post exercises measured the C2 system only, with subordinate units simulating action and passing message traffic and reports through the system. But there were plenty of larger exercises in which actual forces participated. For example, in what we called Reforger exercises, combat and support elements were airlifted from stateside bases into the theater to demonstrate the capacity for rapid reinforcement, then stayed a while, maneuvering alongside European-based units and responding to NATO direction, an exercise revealing much about our readiness. However, force-on-force exercises were expensive, so we limited their scale and frequency.

The standard exercise scenario started with warning of Warsaw Pact movement into forward, jump-off positions. Soviet-style attack featured armored formations arrayed in depth, the breakthrough elements followed by trailing echelons that exploited any opening. The main thrust would be across the North German Plain into Holland. This is the traditional invasion corridor, property Montgomery took in World War II. Together with Belgian, Dutch, and West German ground forces, the Brits still occupied positions astride this route. In the south, where our Army was garrisoned, there was a second attack axis, through the Fulda Gap and into central and southern Germany, aiming eventually to capture Rhine crossings. The way our exercises were played, Pact forces always made rapid progress, we fell back on a series of hastily prepared defenses, and in the end, faced the grim choice of giving up or resorting to nuclear use.

There was something fantastic about these scenarios, but we inhabited an alternate, command-post world in which make-believe events acquired realism and legitimacy. Inside the Bunker, pressure built up—lots of problems to solve, many ways to go wrong—as long days and long nights ran out, leaving no trace of either sunlight or darkness.

For the big exercises, usually three times a year, our four-star leadership showed up at the Bunker. My boss, Gen. John Pauly, the AAFCE and USAFE commander, was a big-airplane guy by trade, with a background in C-130s, but he was smart, knew the business inside out and had good rapport with the Allies. I respected and liked him a lot. The time he spent in the Bunker was his most intense contact with his boss in the Allied chain, the German Army four-star, and I wanted our performance in the air operations center to make him look good. As we were perforce thrown together during these exercises, I watched for any sign he thought things were looking up at the Bunker. He gave no hint he was pleased at what he saw, but I knew it was getting better. Not good . . . better.

Franz-Joseph Schulze, the German Army four-star, was very bright, seeming to know every rock and tree in the Federal Republic and exactly how to defend it. He was also rather volatile, a holy terror for his staff. Schulze could not comprehend the empty-headedness of staff recommendations made to him during exercises. I was insulated a bit since I worked for Pauly, and, anyway, I rather admired Schulze. But it was no fun watching him tear the hide off his own people. Still, if you ever have to defend Germany, send for Schulze.

When he retired, Schulze was replaced by General Doctor F. von Senger und Etterlin, of old European aristocracy, from the Black Forest region. Von Senger had world-class dandruff and lost most of an arm in World War II—the Russian Front, of course—but was one of society's highborn and therefore noticed neither of these conditions. When von Senger came to the Bunker for an orientation, I walked him through Air Force holdings. During the stroll, I paused to introduce a couple of French liaison officers passing us in a hallway, whereupon von Senger said, "Oh, yes, my ancestors have been killing Frenchmen for centuries!"

I got all kinds of visitors at the Bunker. Bobby Beckel, my old friend from Thunderbird days, had been assigned to Europe and came by for the newcomer treatment. Bob switched to the strategic business after his Vietnam tour and had already commanded two wings and been promoted to one-star, passing me in afterburner. SAC had sent him to command its air division in Europe, a holding company for the bombers, tankers, and reconnaissance aircraft that cycled through the theater.

I hadn't seen Bobby for a few years, and when he alighted at our helipad, his first words were "What happened?" By which he meant, of course, how come I was out here in the leafy Hunsrück? What had I done? Whom had I angered? All my friends must be asking the same question. I'd been pushed aside, out of the fight, stuck in this hole in the ground.

Meanwhile, I kept reporting for work at the mineshaft, telling myself this wasn't why I joined the outfit. The real Air Force had left me behind. For the first time, I began thinking about retirement.

Toward the end of our time at Birkenfeld, the Army let a contract to replace windows in our apartment complex with more energy-efficient, double-paned glass. Supposedly to keep dangerous shards from falling into flowerbeds, workmen pounded *in* the windows and casements with German efficiency, producing a fusillade of broken glass and dust throughout the apartment, then came inside and threw the broken glass and wrecked wood *out* the window. We were still finding and cleaning up debris when we departed A Building for our next assignment.

In December 1979, NATO ministers met in Brussels and agreed to modernize our theater nuclear-deterrent capability with Army Pershing II short-range ballistic missiles and USAF ground-launched cruise missiles (GLCMs), these systems seen as an offset for the Russians' newly introduced SS-20. Of course, this constituted an escalation in the Cold War, but the A Building window project made the notion of nuclear war in Central Europe seem somehow more manageable.

Soviet airborne troops landed in Kabul, Afghanistan, on Christmas Day, 1979, ending the period of détente. President Carter canceled our participation in the Moscow Olympic Games. For most of the next nine years, the Soviets maintained a force of about 100,000 in Afghanistan, losing nearly 15,000 of their troops.

I spent a good bit of time at Ramstein in the peace headquarters. The drive took an hour and a half, bad road most of the way. A trip down and back, connected to any business there, kept me away from the Bunker a whole day, something I couldn't afford to do often. Nevertheless, Air Vice-Marshal Kingshot and other AAFCE dignitaries wanted to see me from time to time, and I made the occasional call on General Pauly. I didn't hang around Ramstein trying to catch his attention, but as I reached important decision points in the development of the Bunker I sought an audience and got direction. When I saw him, I was organized and got in and out of his office quickly.

Pauly had a New Year's reception at the club for all officers—a black-tie affair. Ellie and I got dressed up and made the drive to Ramstein. As we went through the receiving line, Pauly pulled me aside and asked, "Would you be interested in going over to England and taking command of the 20th Fighter Wing?"

This had to be a trick question.

I left Börfink Bunker in February 1980, having spent 20 months there, the longest of my eight assignments as a colonel.

Chapter 8

20th Wing

A man should be what he can do.
— Pvt. Robert E. Lee "Prew" Prewitt,
in *From Here to Eternity,* by James Jones

RAF Station Upper Heyford stood at the edge the Cotswolds, 12 road miles north of Oxford, site of the ancient university. In villages around the base, honey-colored local limestone had been used to build churches and cottages, producing a pleasing architectural uniformity. During medieval times, half the wealth of England walked around here on four legs, Cotswold wool being prized above all others and commanding a premium. The speaker of the House of Lords still sat on the woolsack, a symbol of how important the trade was for England.

The 20th Tactical Fighter Wing came here in April 1970. Before the move, the wing had been split, its headquarters and two flying squadrons at Wethersfield, and my old outfit, the 79th Squadron, at Woodbridge. Now combined farther west at Upper Heyford, the squadrons had also converted from F-4s to F-111s, an aircraft with more than enough range to compensate for the increased mileage to Warsaw Pact targets.

Upper Heyford was an older, more established base, the Royal Air Force having been in and out of the place since 1917. Strategic Air Command put some money into the base in the early years of the Cold War, when bombers and tankers pulled alert there. We were now in the middle of a large, NATO-funded construction phase, building individual hardened shelters for each aircraft and reinforced concrete structures to replace the wood and brick buildings that housed essential operations and maintenance facilities. This would make for a much sturdier base, protected as well as could be against conventional or nuclear attack.

The 20th Wing was a storied formation, having inherited the honors of the 20th Fighter Group. The wing's squadrons—the 55th, 77th, and 79th—were among the Air Force's earliest, all veterans of the Great War. As I took over early in 1980, the 20th was also one of our largest wings. Its centerpiece was the flying operation at Heyford, 75 F-111Es with a nuclear-alert mission. In addition, nearly all Air Force activity in the south central UK had been put under the wing, including a large ammunition storage depot at RAF Welford, a major communications hub at RAF Croughton, the dependent school at RAF High Wycombe, and the standby base at RAF Greenham Common, which we kept ready to absorb reinforcements flowing in from the States during exercise or crisis. I had about 5,000 people working for me at Upper Heyford and perhaps another 1,000 scattered among these other bases.

My immediate boss, Maj. Gen. Bill Norris, Third Air Force commander, got his first star at the end of a successful run as commander of the 50th Wing at Hahn Air Base, Germany. Then he'd been moved to Upper Heyford to "help" the 20th. F-111s had arrived in Europe with a flourish, the theater's first true, long-range, all-weather tactical nuclear-delivery system, whereupon the wing flunked its initial NATO tactical evaluation and could not be declared combat ready on schedule, a great humiliation for all concerned. Norris came in, knocked heads together, and subsequently guided the wing through a successful retake. I did not know Norris, meeting him the first time when he came to Upper Heyford for my assumption-of-command ceremony, at which General Pauly officiated. An intense man, Norris took an abiding interest in the 20th Wing. Approaching the end of an Air Force career, he remained compact, idealistic, a warrior type. I got the impression he was unhappy about my showing up to command one of his wings. It was possible Pauly had not consulted him in appointing me, perhaps because the 20th, in the second half of 1979, had crashed four F-111s and lost six of the eight crew members involved. Then, in January 1980, it had lost another, again killing the crew. This is not the sort of record that assures inclusion in the new-commander selection process.

Within a week of my taking command, Norris showed up on short notice, making the three-hour drive over backcountry roads from his headquarters at Mildenhall. At his request, I took him on a windshield tour of the base. He knew what was inside every building, behind every door, and I did not. Repeatedly, he told me to stop the car so he could show me what was important, what had slipped since he'd left, what needed fixing. This was painful and would have been even more so had it not been crystal clear the man delighted in hands-on contact with the mission, mourned having been kicked upstairs, an echelon removed, had an almost physical need to be in the middle of real operations.

At length, we arrived at a small, reinforced concrete building, still under construction. Soon it would be the wing's command center, hardened against attack by conventional or chemical munitions, and therefore my place of business during emergencies, exercises, or active combat operations. For now it was a mess, tools downed in place, every surface filthy, crumpled soft-drink cans and ground-out cigarette ends forming a scum that rode on top the layer of ordinary debris—scrap lumber, chunks of drywall, snippets of wiring, cutoff lengths of tubing—in brief, debased in a way only construction workers have mastered.

The English workday completed, we were alone in the building. At its center, a small, elevated battle cab neared completion. We entered, wiped off metal folding chairs, and, once seated, looked through large, grimy windows at the surrounding disorder. Norris leaned back. "You know, McPeak," he said thoughtfully, "a command post is where a commander does his most important work. In my experience, it shows his personality, his style, his character." He went slowly, choosing his words. "You get a mental picture of a commander just by visiting his command post. If it's not properly organized—not clean, not squared away—if it's empty, if there's nothing going on in there, you learn a lot about a commander."

Norris was a racquetball fanatic. His aide had called beforehand to say he'd be bringing his gym gear and expected a game. After listening to the ways I resembled the unfinished command-post project, I dropped him at Visiting Officers Quarters and went home to change. I looked forward to getting this guy in the court. Turned out he was not that bad a player, a Vince Lombardi type, willing to do anything to win, including cheat, if it wasn't too obvious. I beat him like a drum.

General Norris came to our quarters that evening for dinner, quieted, a nicer person. He picked at his meal, making his own construction project—a carrot fence for the meat, a series of mashed-potato dams. The relationship between us now adjusted, he would henceforth treat me with reserve, even kindness. He never returned to Upper Heyford. I saw him from time to time at his headquarters or at Ramstein when we attended commanders' conferences. But he otherwise limited our contact to the occasional phone call, usually an attractive hash of gruff and gentle advice, except when he read in one of the police blotters forwarded to him daily that my cops had caught some local women in one of the enlisted dormitories. He was death on hard drink and loose women. "Booze and broads," he told me on the phone, "that's poison. No outfit's worth a damn if you can't keep booze and broads out of the barracks." He called at intervals to repeat the theme, but apart from this particular hobbyhorse, stayed off my case.

Following my visit from Norris, I returned to the States for a quick checkout in the F-111. A General Dynamics design, this was the first "variable geometry" combat aircraft to enter service, its wings sweepable from pretty straight (12 degrees) to pretty swept (65 degrees), accommodating a wide range of flying speeds. Variable geometry offers an expensive, complicated, but effective solution to the problem of how to make an airplane that will go fast at both high and low altitude but not gobble up large amounts of fuel and real estate during takeoff and landing. Many would argue the F-111 remains the best combination of speed, payload, and range of any airplane ever built. But it surely was big and heavy, in reality not a fighter but a medium bomber, a replacement for the B-25 of Doolittle's raid. You could light the afterburners and still hold the thing steady while checking engines prior to brake release, which sounds like a good thing but isn't. For any fighter with a decent thrust-to-weight ratio, afterburner will overwhelm the wheel brakes.

The jet featured terrain-following radar (TFR) that could be coupled to the autopilot for hands-off high-speed, low-altitude flight at night or in bad weather. I actually had to do some of this during my checkout at Mountain Home AFB, Idaho, and it scared me silly, even with an experienced instructor sitting close at hand in the much-detested side-by-side cockpit layout. On autopilot, the aircraft would follow terrain contours at 200 feet and, with the wings swept back, at airspeeds above 500 knots. This was bad enough in weather, which usually will give you at least an occasional peek at the ground. But black, dark night or, worse, night weather would keep you on the edge of your seat, which is where you'd better be, given the then-current state of avionics. Once or twice while auto-TFRing at night I (no kidding) saw reflections bounce off dirt on either side, the terrain lit up by the strobing of the aircraft's rotating beacon. It was great when it worked, but quite a few unexplained losses had occurred, F-111s simply not coming back from training sorties.

This was now the second fighter in which I got an abbreviated, "senior officer" checkout. Not good. At 200 feet and 500 knots, in weather or at night, it lightens the load if you've had *all* the academics, *all* the simulator rides, and know *all* about the airplane. However, that would take time I supposedly couldn't spare.

The F-111 had started out as a joint program, Robert McNamara having dragged the Air Force and Navy together on the argument that producing a single airplane for both services would save a ton of money. The contractor actually built seven F-111s for the Navy before they managed to deep-six their participation, opting instead to field the F-14 Tomcat, also a large, variable-geometry fighter, but better suited to their requirements. Though the Navy's F-111 involvement was temporary, the design compromises made necessary by forced jointness were permanent, much reducing the aircraft's overall quality. Had McNamara not outsmarted himself and the services (as well as the country), both we and the Navy would have fielded a much better aircraft at significantly lower total cost.

Aircrews have no choice but to love the airplane they fly. Aside from this small constituency, the F-111 was not popular in the Air Force. It was the only combat aircraft without an official nickname. We called it the Aardvark (or "Vark"), an only modestly affectionate reference to its ungainly form. It was way too big and heavy to have much appeal in the fighter community. The Air Force made SAC accept a few advanced versions, called the FB-111, but it carried too small a payload and was too short-legged to impress the bomber guys. The engines and avionics were a maintenance nightmare, hellishly expensive to keep flying. The Air Force ran through several variants trying to upgrade reliability, the production batches so abbreviated that all of a certain model could be located at one base. For instance, only 94 F-111Es were built, with all the ones then still flying based at Upper Heyford. The 48th Wing at Lakenheath, the other overseas outfit in F-111s, had all the F-111Fs.

While I was at Mountain Home checking out in the Aardvark, my wing back at Upper Heyford lost a jet. A couple of guys from the 77th Squadron let down through cloud and simply ran into the ground. No radio calls, no sign of an emergency.

Any crew loss hurts, but this accident particularly distressed me. I'd never before lost anyone in operations under my control. My sample size might be small, but it included some high-risk activity: gunnery training at Luke, Thunderbird opposing solo work, the Misty FACs. So this was the first aircrew loss for which I had chain-of-command responsibility, and here I was in beautiful, downtown Mountain Home, Idaho.

It didn't help that the investigation led nowhere, the cause of the accident never determined.

A Rube Goldberg special, the F-111 aircrew-ejection system turned out to be much worse than even the complicated Martin-Baker seat in the F-4. Some bright person figured that the crew needed protection during high-speed ejection—certainly correct—but he also decided to make the whole cockpit and a big chunk of structure around it into an escape capsule, akin to something from the space program. Getting all this separated from the airplane and then deposited safely on land or in water required sequential miracles. I sincerely hoped I'd never have to use it.

Back home at Upper Heyford, I was absolutely delighted to be running a wing. A wing is the lowest management level where all the pieces come together to produce an organization for air fighting, making command of a combat wing the best job in the Air Force. Combining the human talent and material potential in just the right way constituted the wing commander's challenge, and from the first day, I felt as though I knew exactly what to do.

I had very good people at Heyford. My vice-commander at the start was Col. Chris D. "Dan" Wright, an experienced fighter jock and real professional. Like many others, including the celebrated Francis Gary Powers, Dan had left the Air Force for a while to fly U-2s with another government organization, in an arrangement that returned him to us at the end of that tour. Talented and wonderful with people, Dan was senior to me by date of rank and probably had been General Norris's choice to take the wing. Now passed over for command, he'd have to be reassigned. He stayed while I went stateside for my F-111 checkout, and briefly afterward. I was happy for his help. Col. (later, Maj. Gen.) Fred Nelson, a hard worker, commanded the combat support group. In due course, Fred succeeded me as 20th Wing commander. The deputy for operations was Col. (later, Lt. Gen.) Dale Thompson. My hospital commander, Lt. Col. Chip Roadman, would rise to three stars and leadership of the Air Force's medical establishment as our surgeon general. Lt. Col. John Lorber led the 79th Squadron. A future four-star, he was simply a great squadron commander, outstanding in every dimension, his people ready to lie down in front of a train for him.

Flying is fun, even in a bomber like the F-111. I especially enjoyed going up to Scotland, one of the few spots in Europe where built-up areas could be left behind, lovely country for "nap of the earth" flying. And it was sort of fun to see whether I could make this clumsy, giant airplane do decent eight-point rolls.

My predecessor as wing commander had averaged one sortie a month, always with an instructor in the right seat. He was a fine officer, but the core mission of the organization was to fly and fight, and his approach sent a certain signal about leadership to the crew force.

Leadership has to do with people and, in particular, getting them to perform. It is the supremely active role, about building a team, calling signals, achieving a result—with *outputs*. Management, on the other hand, has to do with things—budget, real property, equipment, inventory. (Where it concerns people, it is a question of *human resources* or *head count*.) Management is a much-maligned undertaking, seeming so passive, so aimed at regulating *inputs*.

Thus, leadership reigns supreme over management in all walks of life, but the eclipse is most total in the profession of arms, where activity, even the image of activity, carries outsized importance. Napoleon is supposed to have indicted the British as a "nation of shopkeepers," unfit to join him in battle, and in military life there is still something a little suspect about number crunching, keeping the in-basket empty, starting meetings on time.

In small units, it's certainly leadership that's wanted. As Sherman is supposed to have said, the captain *is* the company. At the lower levels of an organization, problems may be complicated, but solutions are usually simple, handled in person and on the spot. But as the size of the outfit grows, the 100 percent leadership model falls apart. In large organizations, slapdash administration will fatally undercut even the strongest leadership. Those annoying inputs had better be managed.

That said, appearances matter, so senior officers are well advised to do their management chores out of sight, even after normal duty hours. In daylight, attend to leadership—leadership by walking around and pushing doors open, leadership by looking and *seeing*, leadership by hands-on performance of the unit's mission, and especially leadership by teaching. Counting preparation, I spent perhaps a third of my time explaining to groups of people what we were trying to do and convincing them it was important. Leadership involves establishing a shared commitment to the organization's goals. Sitting in the office will not get this done.

Still, no real tension exists between leadership and management. They are not binary alternatives, but two aspects of the same job. A commander must sit in the office. Just be sure to do it at night.

I scheduled myself to fly once a week, and always with a naviga-tor, preferably the most inexperienced or junior available.

Our quarters were large, a neoclassical redbrick. The RAF built the place just after World War I and configured it for life in the colonial era. The backyard contained the remnant of a lawn ten-nis court. There was a gardener who seemed to have been with the house forever. Buzzers connected bedrooms to kitchen, so help could be summoned from below. (We reversed the system so Ellie could get Brian down to dinner.) The place was something of a white ele-phant, a maintenance headache. The monster boiler, a relic that had to be coerced into service, supplied hot water and heated the living area. Luckily, base civil engineers had retained the ser-vices of the only person in those isles who could make it work. One nice feature: a large electric transformer. Moving around Europe, we'd carried our own portable transformers to convert wall plug 50-cycle to the 60-cycle needed by American-made appliances. We could now set these aside for a while, the central device transform-ing all current coming into the house.

As with most communities, military organizations move and act by willing consensus. But the desired aim point is seldom obvious. Accordingly, if I had to choose one rule for large unit leadership, it would be this: make sure everybody knows what you want done.

At work, early in the morning, *good* people think about what must be done to accomplish the mission. When they're happy on that score, they work on things they enjoy or are in the habit of doing. With *really good* people, there's lots of overlap between these two sets of priorities. The boss's to-do list is the last one people pay attention to. But a good boss plays a trick, making his list also redundant of list one. So, why even have a list? Because your *very best people* will make a special effort to work the boss's problem.

The power to establish priorities is therefore leadership's secret weapon. Early in my tenure at Upper Heyford, I published a list:

Protect Our Deterrent Assets
Exploit Readiness Opportunities
Plan Our Facilities Future
Improve Services to People
Keep the Base Clean

I had only five priorities, kept the sentences short, started every line with a verb. The list was simple even though the issues were complex. For instance, our "deterrent assets" were aircraft, the men who launched and flew them, and the conventional and nuclear munitions stored on the base. I didn't want to lose any of these assets. Exactly how to "not lose" them is a problem requiring a lifetime of study, but I could state the priority and make sure everyone understood it was number one.

As we were in the middle of a very expensive construction program to harden aircraft shelters and other facilities providing essential wartime support, I thought we should figure out how to use the new structures to enhance fighting qualities. We had a "readiness opportunity" that needed to be thought about and exploited. Again, this was anything but a simple problem, but putting it in simplest terms and high on the list meant everybody could take a crack at solving a piece of it.

The other priorities were straightforward, goals everybody in the wing could understand and act on.

I put this priorities list in the base newspaper, passed it around at meetings, mounted a framed version on my office wall. Smart squadron commanders slid the list under Plexiglas protecting their desktops. To make sure I seemed reasonably flexible, I claimed the list would be revised every six months, but I knew these priorities would endure. When I left the wing after sixteen months, not one word had changed.

Over the years, I saw many such lists. Almost always they were counterproductive: too long, obvious committee work, bloated by bureaucrat-speak. They often suffered from not wanting to leave out anything important, and so stated too many priorities, the exact equivalent of having none.

Paying attention to what Bill Norris had said, I decorated the command post battle cab so it reflected my taste, hanging plaques of subordinate squadrons and giving pride of place to the flying organizations—the 55th, 77th, and 79th. I discovered these plaques were not standardized, each of different manufacture, size, and shape. By contrast, a visit to any RAF station anywhere in the world will put on display squadron plaques produced to identical design standards. I ended up having a uniform set made up in our civil engineer carpentry shops.

About 10 miles from the base, near the village of Woodstock, Queen Anne had sponsored construction of a country house for John Churchill, supposedly to be built at her expense. Born into a family that included high-ranking members of English society, Churchill himself was of the gentry rather than aristocracy. His creation as 1st Duke of Marlborough and the gift of a house were the rewards of a grateful nation for saving Europe from French domination, 70 years before our Declaration of Independence. The name of the house, Blenheim Palace, memorializes Marlborough's most famous victory.

The duke continued to serve his country overseas after the Battle of Blenheim, piling victory on victory and becoming quite popular, with the predictable result that plots hatched against him. It's a complicated story, but in the end much of the money promised for building Blenheim Palace never arrived, leaving the duke with a debt of about 45,000 pounds sterling owed to his architect, masons, carpenters, and the like. He never saw the place completed.

The palace had an up-and-down history over the years, and

the dukedom was nearly bankrupt when Charles Richard John Spencer-Churchill, the 9th Duke, married Consuelo Vanderbilt. The dowry she brought saved the place. But Consuelo was never happy. When she left Charles, another American, Gladys Deacon, took her place. This marriage, too, held little joy, the second duchess positioning a revolver next to her plate when the couple dined alone.

Winston Churchill was born at the palace. Perhaps Britain's most famous prime minister, he liked to be known as the Great Commoner, though the 1st Duke certainly had the better claim to this description. Although a schemer, John Churchill rose by talent and hard work. No doubt Winston did the same. Still, nobody born upstairs in Blenheim Palace should be called a commoner.

Following his father's precedent, Sir Winston shortened his legal surname, Spencer-Churchill, but it reminds us of a connection to the family that foaled Lady Diana Spencer. Now, in the early months of 1981, she was engaged to Charles, Prince of Wales and heir to the throne. A breathless press followed the courtship. One of the less damaging stories claimed she had twice failed her O levels; that is, by our standards, she hadn't finished high school. But she was tall—at 5 feet 10 inches, casting a shadow on Charles in more ways than one—and very pretty, well on her way to becoming the preeminent celebrity of her time.

She and Charles married in July 1981, a month after we departed for a new assignment in Germany. That marriage didn't work either, but Lady Di pulled a reverse Consuelo, getting a lump-sum settlement of 17 million pounds on divorce.

Blenheim Palace was open to the public. A tour of the house and its grounds, followed by lunch at the Bear in Woodstock, was part of the standard package we offered visitors. Ellie had many such sorties to her credit. I never got to see the place. One of the few characteristics the 1st Duke and I might have shared was a preoccupation with overseas military duties.

The role of the military wife has evolved over the years, thank goodness. One has the impression that in the old days, a commander's wife exercised dominion over subordinate wives, even subordinates themselves. If so, things were better now than when John Wayne rode into Fort Apache. Protocol—some published, much unspoken—continued to constrain to some degree the social activity of spouses, but being a Cold War commander's wife was more like an unpaid full-time job than sitting atop some pecking order, especially overseas. Here, officers' wives' clubs, NCO wives' clubs, thrift shops, schools, and hospitals all provided essential community support; all relied on volunteer help; and, as one might expect, all were potential incubators for friction that could migrate quickly to the workplace. Often, the action of a thoughtful commander's wife could relax tensions, though I'd seen the reverse happen more than once. At a minimum, a commander's wife could subvert much of what he was trying to get done, like Penelope, undoing the knitting by night. I was lucky Ellie handled the problem with intelligence and a fair dose of finesse.

In London, the RAF Club had a good address on Piccadilly, near Hyde Park. I accepted an invitation to join. Staying there was inexpensive, cost now more a factor for us than during the early '60s, when the pound-dollar relationship meant, on a lieutenant's pay, we could afford to buy or do just about anything we wanted. The club had a nice atmosphere, lots of hired help, meeting rooms hushed and filled with memorabilia. The food was solid English fare, but nothing's perfect.

The Air Force had four wings in the UK, and I hit on the idea of getting the commanders together in London for an evening out. We all signed up to stay at the RAF Club and have a meal in Soho at a place called the Gay Hussar. Following dinner, we headed to Covent Garden for an evening at the theater. The eight of us were scarcely seated when a bomb threat emptied the building. IRA terrorists, or so we were told.

The daily flying schedule was meant to keep individual aircrews mission ready, but we fought as a wing so, periodically, we suspended normal flying and trained collectively for combat and for the regular visits of inspection teams from higher headquarters.

This was the way a wing exercise worked: We started by scrambling the aircraft on Victor Alert—a dozen of them, each loaded with two or three nuclear bombs. We always did this first because it tested no-notice reaction time. The alert crews had to dress quickly, run to aircraft, strap in and start engines. We hacked the clock and added five minutes for taxi and takeoff. Total elapsed time to wheels up must be under 15 minutes for all aircraft, or we failed the exercise before it was properly begun.

Immediately, we recalled everybody to duty stations using rosters that cascaded phone calls through each squadron. Many of our people lived off base in surrounding communities, and we rousted them out of bed—these exercises seemed always to kick off at night—and hurried them back. We needed to know how long it took to go from a standing start to ready for war. Once we'd accounted for everybody, we organized 12-hour shifts and sent half the people home.

Then followed a period of conventional combat. We "generated" aircraft; that is, we fueled, serviced oxygen and other systems, loaded munitions, inspected and prepared for launch. Normally, a snapshot of the wing would show as many as half our aircraft "broken" for some reason—perhaps maintenance in progress, or lack of a serviceable part to replace some piece of faulty equipment. Now we cleaned out lockers, emptied warehouses and strained hard to get all our jets fit to fly. Meanwhile, squadrons received target assignments, provoking a flurry of aircrew planning that blended intelligence estimates, weather, tactics, and wartime routing and reporting procedures.

So, generating the wing and bringing it to the highest readiness state made for a period of feverish activity, much of it at night or in bad weather, with everyone in the wing working hard, and every action watched and graded. Then we called time-out, downloaded and returned real munitions to the conventional weapon storage area, replaced them with dispensers of practice munitions, and the war started. Aircraft launched, to the degree feasible, using practices that replicated wartime rather than normal operations. (For instance, we might do everything with visual signals rather than radio transmissions, which an enemy could intercept.) Crews flew combat-profile missions to virtual targets and on the way home dropped in at gunnery ranges where they released and scored practice bombs. Evaluators flew along and graded aircrew performance at every stage.

Usually, the period of mock conventional war would extend over three days. During this time we responded to a variety of simulated emergencies—ground attacks, air attacks, runway cratering, fuel fires, mass casualties, nuclear accidents, and so forth—all of which tested our security force, civil engineers, fire department, and hospital. Every airman was involved, even those with the most sedentary daily jobs, because each had a backup responsibility to train and augment first responders. Even under normal conditions, this kind of thing could be exhausting, but we spent much of the three-day period in heavy, rubberized chem/bio suits and wearing gas masks, apparel that increased fatigue and made duty shifts seem considerably longer than 12 hours.

Finally, we would "lose" the conventional war and have to escalate. We'd already exercised the alert aircraft, so now we loaded out the whole wing, every jet we had, with nuclear weapons. This meant opening up a separate storage area, wheeling these special bombs out of their igloos, putting together a convoy of distinctive trailers that held the weapons and parading past each aircraft shelter to drop off laden trailers as we went. This nuclear weapon distribution parade was called an elephant walk. Again, we took a time hack because the wing had to be able to generate for nuclear operations within strict time limits. After loading every aircraft, we again downloaded the real weapons, put them back in storage—a reverse elephant walk—and again reconfigured with practice bombs. Then we exercised the communications protocols for selective and general nuclear release—the fail-safe system— and aircrews launched for a final sortie to the bombing range, again keeping track of scores. At length, we terminated the exercise, evaluators wrote a report, and in a few hours we debriefed commanders and staff, emphasizing lessons learned and items we had to work harder on. Obviously, these exercises were highly stylized because of a risk profile we had to keep under control. The form was theme and variations; there wasn't much room for improvisation.

I spent most of every exercise in the battle cab, the glassed-off enclosure in the middle of the command post. An array of status boards faced me, so I could track the condition of all critical assets in the wing. Naturally, these included aircrews, aircraft, munitions, fuel, and spare parts, but there were also hundreds of other items not so obvious: liquid oxygen, tow bars, aircraft ladders. How much or how many of each did we have? Where were they? What about food and water? Were the dining halls still up and operating? What could we get out of the commissary? How many fire trucks were available for deployment? Front-loaders? Backhoes? Sweepers? When we came under simulated chemical attack, how many people were protected? In which shelters? Who were they? How soon could we decontaminate and get back in business?

Occasionally I left the command post to visit important work centers, checking action on the spot, but mostly I kept a watchful eye from the battle cab, intervening by telephone or radio as needed to push the exercise along. Massing and focusing the efforts of the wing required both experience and skill. My career was rich in the right experience, and, as luck would have it, I had a knack for conducting the orchestra.

We had nearly everything needed to fight a war on our own: airplanes, crews, fuel, munitions, the whole heavy impedimenta of industrial conflict. In most respects, higher headquarters was a bother, and I visualized the good fortune of communications failure. When I inspected the base's telephone infrastructure, this seemed possible, even likely. Incoming phone calls were routed through a venerable, PBX-style switchboard the Brits had liberated from the Germans and removed to the UK in the immediate aftermath of World War II. Metal swastikas adorned the sides of this antique. It was slow, manpower intensive, and, unhappily, quite reliable.

Though I needed little outside support, the exception was crucial. I had to have intelligence, especially what was in my view by far the most important of its several varieties: targeting information. We relied entirely on higher headquarters to tell us what to attack. Were the phone to go dead, we could still fight. But who?

Gen. Bernard Rogers, NATO's current SACEUR, visited the base from time to time. A former Rhodes scholar, he flew in for the occasional alumni event at Oxford. We put him up in VIP quarters, nice enough but, as we know, the Brits consider modern plumbing effete. At the end of his first visit, I was drawn aside by Rogers's aide, who reported the general was not happy with the force, direction, and quantity of water delivered during his morning shower. Temperature was OK. I made a personal inspection, confirming SACEUR's observations. Over time, hard water would close off the small holes in the showerhead. Before each of his future returns, I visited the bathroom, remedying the situation with a straight pin.

Upper Heyford had hundreds of nuclear weapons stored on base, each with a potential yield far in excess of the Hiroshima bomb. We kept them apart from conventional munitions, in special bunkers, behind double fencing and a sophisticated lighting and monitoring apparatus, but because the weapons required periodic maintenance, people got access to them routinely. Moreover, the bombs themselves moved in and out of the facility all the time. Aircraft took turns on alert, just like aircrews, so we were constantly uploading and downloading, delivering and returning live nuclear munitions. Maybe our highest exposure came during wing exercises, when we staged the elephant walk, flushing perhaps half our weapons out of storage to configure the entire wing for nuclear war.

We had complicated rules for doing all this, designed to build in maximum safety and security. And if someone got unauthorized access to one of the things, he'd have a hard time making it go off. Still, I worried a good bit about these nuclear weapons. I could do everything else perfectly, and it wouldn't matter much if I lost track of even one little nuke. So, like the bombs themselves, I was in and out of the special storage facility all the time, including the middle of the night. I rode shotgun on weapon convoys. I did not meet privately with every airman in the wing but made an exception for security policemen selected and specially trained for guard duty in the nuclear storage facility. They all got to come by my office for a little chat before their first duty tour.

About 500 teenagers of both sexes attended high school at RAF High Wycombe. They came from all over Europe, children of military and Foreign Service personnel stationed at locations too small to have their own school. We had a lieutenant colonel and small administrative staff stationed there in support of the school and its civilian faculty. In theory, the boys and girls lived in separate dormitories. The lieutenant colonel reported any noteworthy incident—these reports coming regularly—and I drove over on occasion to assess the damage.

If you ever want full-time work, try keeping 500 teenage boys and girls, living in adjoining dormitories, separated.

Construction of the hardened aircraft shelters neared completion. Huge, ponderous, they squatted and thrust meter-thick, steel-reinforced concrete arches upward, proof against any high explosive except a direct hit. If they weathered nothing more than the elements, they'd be standing when Stonehenge was flat, a curiosity some far-future archeologist would credit to exceedingly strange tribal rites. For now, they stuck out against the English heath, 72 beached, chalk-white whales. At least their arrangement followed no pattern. We'd scattered and plumped them down at random angles to break up the profile. Moreover, headquarters had let a contract to a Belgian firm to stain the shelters, tone down their pallor, make them blend with surroundings.

The Belgians showed up and sprayed away. I inspected the first result and couldn't believe what I saw. Glistening with a purple sheen that dried to nearly coal black, the shelters were, if anything, more conspicuous after painting—the polar opposite of the desired outcome. I stopped work and called the head civil engineer (a one-star) at headquarters. Four days of telephone haggling ensued, the issue being who's in charge around here. At length I was stood at attention and told to fly airplanes and they'd paint shelters.

To cope with the industrial eyesore and newly created bomb magnet, I asked my own civil engineers to invent a tree-planting program. It turned out Her Majesty's foresters gave away larch and Scotch pine saplings, if we agreed to stick them in the dirt. We planted many thousands, creating nascent copses all over the aerodrome and breaking up our silhouette. It was an investment, since each year the trees would give better cover, but they began to pay off immediately, much reducing our target signature.

The RAF held title to the base at Upper Heyford and kept a landlord there, Wing Commander Joe Shotten, a fine officer. By contrast with the Spanish, the Brits made it easy to be on their real estate. Much more relaxed and hands-off, they let us treat the place as though it were our own.

Joe Shotten joined me on our Friendship Committee, made up of local dignitaries I wined and dined and tried to keep happy. In general, Anglo-American relations were quite good, my only problem relating to aircraft noise.

A typical stateside Air Force base will have title to thousands of acres. But NATO bases were usually much smaller, kind of stationary aircraft carriers. The noise from aircraft engines operating above idle RPM will surely vibrate local glassware. At Upper Heyford, our normal takeoff and landing patterns ran right across some otherwise pastoral English villages, with pastoral English names, like Steeple Aston. The good citizens of Steeple Aston rang me up often.

Such a community relations problem would appear ready-made for action by the Friendship Committee, but ours wasn't doing much. Now mostly in their seventies, the members had served seemingly since the days of the Disraeli government. They were happy to come to Fourth of July garden parties but were otherwise dormant. I decided to honor them with a party, thank them for distinguished service, give them nice going-away gifts and recruit some new blood—a good move, as it turned out, because I got a younger, more active Friendship Committee. However, it didn't eliminate, or even markedly attenuate, noise complaints. I did everything short of compromising flight safety, but only base closure would solve the noise problem.

In March 1981, we lost another F-111. It diverted in bad weather into RAF Fairford. Serviced and turned around, the pilot didn't like what he saw on takeoff, aborted, ran off the concrete, and collapsed the landing gear. Nobody was hurt, but the jet was a fixer-upper, so we boxed it up and sent it back for a refund.

The facilities construction program gave me an opportunity to bulldoze many old buildings around the base. If you don't do this, people will move into their new building, then expand back into the old one. Early in my assignment at Heyford, I found small, decrepit, locked buildings—nobody knew where the keys were. I started kicking in doors. These buildings always contained a dog's breakfast of obsolete parts, dated administrative records, broken furniture—just plain junk.

The problem with junk is it fills up the field of view, making you think you have everything you need. Then a real requirement comes along, and you have nothing but junk. Getting rid of the junk may show the cupboard is pretty bare, something you'd better know before the war starts.

All around the base we had stacks of wooden pallets. Arriving freight provided more pallets daily, free of charge. We also had a surplus of empty 55-gallon drums. Additionally, the giant cable-spool bird flew over the base at regular intervals and left droppings. Pallets, 55-gallon drums, and depleted cable spools are inherently stealthy, examples of physical objects that accumulate and blend by magic into surroundings, becoming so commonplace no one notices them. I took many officers and NCOs around to the back of their buildings to show them the deposited pallets, empty 55-gallon drums, and derelict cable spools—junk mines waiting to be quarried.

The ground-launched cruise missile (GLCM) was coming to NATO. Already, the Russians had modernized their intermediate-range nuclear force (INF) with a ballistic missile, the SS-20, first tested in 1974, then deployed in 1977. This impelled the Allies to replace the Army's Pershing I with the improved Pershing II, and with GLCM, the Air Force version of the Navy's Tomahawk cruise missile.

After spending many dollars and much political capital, we would eventually trade off Pershing II and GLCM for the SS-20 in 1987, when Ronald Reagan and Mikhail Gorbachev signed the INF Treaty, the event signaling a breakthrough in arms control and setting course for the end of the Cold War. Just then, however, GLCM deployment was raising a storm of anti-American, anti-nuclear sentiment all across Europe.

Already bedded down on the Continent, GLCM headed for the UK. The story gained currency that it would become part of the 20th Wing, and the public assumed this meant Upper Heyford. In fact, a connection did exist, since the actual deployment site was Greenham Common, one of the outlying bases under my command. To protect Greenham, we neither confirmed nor denied the report that GLCM was coming to Upper Heyford, which had the practical effect of confirming it, so Heyford became the early target of popular unrest.

On 17 May 1980, the anti-GLCM forces organized a march on Upper Heyford, easy to do since the Queen's Highway ran smack through the middle of the base and nearby Oxford University was a rent-a-crowd outlet. The Thames Valley Constabulary responded, posting bobbies at intervals along the road. We Yanks stayed out of sight, leaving it to the Brits, who were masterful at handling this sort of thing, their experience running all the way back to the most famous such event, the 1958 march from Hyde Park to Aldermaston. That one featured Bertrand Russell, a newly organized Campaign for Nuclear Disarmament, and happened so long ago I was in flying school at Hondo.

On the day of the protest, I took up a post atop a building next to the highway. Rumor had it that the film actress Julie Christie would be there, and I was curious, hoping to see this lady in the flesh. The parade wandered by, a strange, even bizarre, collection, but quite peaceful. Many protesters had spent the night at a makeshift campsite a mile or so north of the base. I watched closely but could not pick out Miss Christie, even with binoculars.

BBC television covered the story that evening, complete with film footage showing Julie Christie in the front ranks. Recognizable at once when highlighted, she had overnighted at the camp and paraded without benefit of cosmetics, her appearance so altered I had not recognized her. No doubt, she was a beautiful woman, but bone structure is not always enough.

In due course, we announced that GLCM would be deployed not at Upper Heyford but at Greenham Common. Stunned, the antinuclear movement shook its head clear and adjusted the aim point. On 5 September 1981, the Greenham Common Women's Peace

Camp was set up just outside the base's perimeter fence, the women living rough, like Julie Christie, in a protest that long outlasted the demise of both GLCM and the SS-20. When, at the turn of the century, the camp was at last abandoned, the Western Berkshire District Council gave planning permission to establish a historic site at the spot.

I set up what I called the Radar Committee, meeting monthly. It included the vice-commander (in his role as inspector general for complaints), the senior enlisted adviser, chaplain, security police squadron commander, judge advocate (JAG), and the heads of hospital sections that ran drug and alcohol abuse and weight-control programs—in short, everybody who did any counseling. The idea was to track the caseload of each agency and provide an information clearinghouse. Some of the people around the table had confidentiality concerns, which I respected. However, this was not a meeting aimed at administrative or disciplinary action. It seemed intrusive, paternalistic, Big Brother in action, and it was, but even a great organization, and the 20th Wing was one of the best, always has people who need help. I wanted those responsible for delivering assistance, including me, to see all the early warning signs.

Twice a year, the USAFE commander called subordinates together for a conference at Ramstein. Commanders of the numbered air forces and of all the large wings attended, together with the leadership from many smaller wings and independent groups. A lot of business got done. The big boss had a chance to give instruction on major issues facing the command. We listened to guest speakers, often senior officers from the Air Staff. There was much social and sports contact. I considered golf a sissy game, but someone always wanted to play handball or racquetball. Mostly this conference gave us a chance to get to know our counterparts, an elite group of people who understood the small triumphs and agonies that came with running Air Force operations at the point of attack.

Charlie Gabriel, who had replaced John Pauly as the head of USAFE, hit on the idea that at each meeting one of us would give a little speech about a mistake he had made and what he'd done about it. The first victim was Col. Mark Anderson, whom I'd known when he was a brand-new lieutenant at Lakenheath. A fine officer (later, a three-star and inspector general of the Air Force), Mark commanded the 36th Wing (F-15s) at Bitburg. He talked about a bonehead mistake he'd made in aircrew supervision. Gabriel ate it up. To Charlie's credit, this would never hurt Anderson.

Though I had plenty of material to draw from, I managed to avoid giving one of these speeches. Confession may be good for the soul, but I'll take the rubber-hose treatment anytime.

In late summer of 1980, Gen. Lew Allen, the Air Force chief of staff, visited Upper Heyford, bringing along a contingent of Air Staff luminaries. We had a regular drill for visitors, including a program for wives (hospital, thrift shop, wives clubs, topped off by the show-stopping trip to Blenheim Palace). The initial part of the visit and the overnight portion went well. To begin our second day together, I planned to take General Allen to breakfast at our enlisted dining hall. Gary Pfingston, a seasoned chief master sergeant with a background in aircraft maintenance, was the 20th Wing's senior enlisted adviser, and therefore my right-hand man on matters concerning welfare of the enlisted force. He offered to vet the airmen who would eat with us, proposing to stack the deck with the Airman of the Quarter, the Outstanding Crew Chief designee, and so forth, but I said no, General Allen and I would just go through the line and sit with whoever showed up.

I sat next to the chief of staff. Across the table sat a first-term airman assigned to the security police squadron. General Allen asked him how he liked it here at Heyford. The guy said it was awful, horrible. We practiced wartime operations constantly; he was out in the cold and dark, staring at chain-link fence, no real action, rain in the face. The chow they delivered was already cold, time he got any.

I about dropped my fork on the floor, seeing a 20-plus-year career disappear into the sunset, but Allen was at bottom a scientist who had not spent much time with troops, and he seemed to take it in stride, maybe thinking this was a normal response. I managed to slip in a leading question or two, drawing from the airman that he was *reenlisting* in the Air Force; that he'd *voluntarily* extended his tour to spend an additional year at Upper Heyford; that he had heard the bus delivering hot (or at least formerly hot) food during exercises had been set up at my initiative (and against Air Force food-handling regulations), *much improving* support previously provided to security posts. I switched the conversation to another, more positive tablemate and by the end of breakfast, may have recovered, partially.

Make a note: on matters like this, pay attention to what your senior enlisted adviser says.

Christmas Day 1980, I got a phone call from Charlie Gabriel, who told me I was on the list for promotion to one-star. This was not entirely a surprise, since the 20th was one of those big wings where we tested colonels. It was nonetheless great news. The Air Force had 6,000 or so colonels on active duty in the late 1970s, early 1980s, and maybe 50 a year made brigadier general.

Many able colonels were promoted alongside me on the list published in January 1981. I'd continue to cross paths with several of them: Michael P. C. Carns, commanding the 57th Fighter Weapons Wing at Nellis AFB; Michael J. Dugan, commanding the 23rd Tactical Fighter Wing at England AFB; and Craven C. "Buck" Rogers Jr., serving as the military assistant to the secretary of the Air Force.

Gabriel also told me I'd have to give up the 20th Wing and come to Ramstein to be his chief of staff, which was not so great.

Looking back, I saw how well a decade of the most varied flying experience had prepared me to use an airplane in combat. I'd spent time as a line pilot in two squadrons, been both frightened and hardened by every kind of aerial incident, flown in good weather and bad, served as a gunnery instructor, spent a couple of years doing air shows, duty at least as testing and dangerous as any war I was likely to see. No human agency had been responsible for what amounted to the best possible preparation. More like dumb luck. I got to the fight late but, for whatever reason and by whatever method, I got there in just the right condition: alert but relaxed.

Then another decade of experience, again accrued seemingly without purposeful design, had given me the most excellent preparation to command a wing. I'd worked as assistant director of a fighter wing's operations, run a support group, served as a wing vice-commander. My time at Börfink Bunker gave me both big picture and fine detail about how wings would be used in a theater of operations. Finally, by some incredible stroke of luck, I'd been given a wing of my own to run. Only a handful of people ever make the transition from what they want to do to what they're meant to do, but here, at the 20th Wing and in my 23rd year of service, I was in exactly the right spot.

And I got to do it for 16 months.

Nearly all general officer jobs are too small—the remaining few, too big. Being a wing commander was just right, the last important Air Force position I held that let me believe I knew precisely what I was doing.

Logbook: Upper Heyford, 1980–81

| F-111A/E | 153.6 |

Chapter 9

Ramstein

. . . victory smiles upon those who anticipate the changes in the character of war, not upon those who wait to adapt themselves after the changes occur.
　　　　　—Giulio Douhet, *The Command of the Air*

Charlie Gabriel had been a good athlete at West Point and went on to score a couple of MiG kills in Korea. He was smart, maybe shrewd rather than cerebral, and secure about his manhood. His leadership style was to be patient with people, but keep track. He was a good guy, the sort you go the extra mile for because you don't want to let him down.

I took up duties as Gabriel's chief of staff on 1 June 1981. The work did not require much imagination. I had no real authority over the staff since the deputies and assistants reported directly to the boss, not through me. I sat atop the paperwork flow, and Gabriel seemed to appreciate my help with the grammar and spelling.

Gabriel had gathered a first-rate team to work in his front office. This was especially true of his officer aide, Maj. Ralph E. "Ed"

Eberhart, a preternaturally talented wingman who kept Gabriel's six o'clock clear.[8] I helped where I could.

Ramstein was the headquarters site for both USAFE, the national, administrative command, and AAFCE, the Allied, war-fighting command. The organizations occupied wings of the same building, and Gabriel went back and forth freely, but a USAFE building pass would not get you into AAFCE, and vice versa. The two staffs were strictly separate and capable of getting cross-ways with each other. Because of my prior service in AAFCE, I understood what both sides were up to and tried to keep Gabriel's national, USAFE actions consistent with what he did on the AAFCE, Alliance side. I also enjoyed renewing contact with many friends in the Allied headquarters.

Someone parked a Volkswagen Beetle overnight near the front steps of our headquarters, and in the early morning of 31 August, it exploded. I was still at home, dawdling over breakfast. From more than a kilometer away, the blast knocked flower boxes off our windowsills. Maj. Gen. Joe Moore, newly arrived as USAFE's deputy for operations, was badly wounded entering the building. Joe was an old friend who had succeeded Neil Eddins as Thunderbird lead in 1969. He came to work earlier than most, so he was the only serious casualty, though 20 others received minor injuries. A few minutes later and the explosion would have caught a lot more of us. Joe Moore spent a week in the hospital and returned to duty, limping a bit.

It's amazing how much damage a Volkswagen and a few liters of fertilizer can do. The command's front offices, including Gabriel's

---

8 Later, as a four-star general, Ed would work his way through a series of high-level postings, including vice chief of staff, commander of Air Combat Command (the successor to Tactical Air Command), commander of Air Force and US Space Command, commander of North American Aerospace Defense Command (NORAD), and finally first commander of the US Northern Command.

and mine, were completely shattered. The entire building was nearly destroyed. It didn't look so bad from the outside, but load-bearing structures throughout had sustained major damage.

The Red Army Faction, successor to the Baader-Meinhof Gang that had metastasized out of the 1960s student protest movement, took credit for the attack. No longer much to brag about—a total strength of maybe 10 people—the organization certainly had a knack for expressing citizenship concerns in an eye-catching way. In 1979, they took a shot at Al Haig, then SACEUR, narrowly missing him. Shortly after bombing our building, they struck again at Heidelberg, launching a rocket through the rear window of Gen. Fritz Kroesen's staff car, with him in it. Kroesen was Gabriel's counterpart as commander of the US Army in Europe. Near the end of 1981, down in Italy, the Red Brigades, Axis ally of the Red Army Faction, kidnapped Army brigadier general James Dozier, holding him for 42 days.

Terrorists were beginning something like a war on us. Here in Europe, we were on the conflict's margins. At this place, and at least for the moment, the local opposition was quaint, out of date, the residue of a toothless Marxism. The main battleground was the Middle East. When Jimmy Carter allowed the exiled Shah of Iran to come to the United States for medical treatment, radicals in Tehran seized our embassy, took 66 diplomats hostage and held most of them for 444 days, a drama that accounted, as much as any single factor, for Carter's reelection defeat. Thus, 4 November 1979, the beginning of the Iran hostage crisis, has a fair claim as the starting date for what some would eventually call the War on Terror, or the Long War.

Americans were not the only casualties; in fact, the terrorists killed many more who were related to them by blood or religion, including for instance Anwar Sadat. Nevertheless, for at least a generation, we were a special target. In April 1983, a suicide bomber in a pickup truck blew up our embassy in Beirut, killing

63 people, including the CIA's director for the Middle East. Later that year, another truck bomber attacked the Marine barracks in Beirut, killing nearly 250, the biggest one-day loss of Marines since Iwo Jima. (We often forget the coordinated attack, six kilometers away and 20 seconds later, that killed 58 French paratroopers.) In April 1984, attackers bombed a restaurant near Torrejon, Spain, killing 18 airmen and wounding 83 people. A series of spectacular airline hijackings took place. The format was established in 1985, when two Hezbollah terrorists took over TWA Flight 847, en route from Athens to Rome, forcing it to Beirut. They held eight crew members and 145 passengers for 17 days, killed one captive, a US sailor, and released their hostages only after Israel freed 435 Lebanese and Palestinian prisoners. Four members of the Palestinian Liberation Front captured the Italian cruise liner Achille Lauro in October 1985, taking 700 hostages and murdering one American passenger before Egypt offered the terrorists safe haven. In 1993, a car bomb exploded in the underground garage of New York City's World Trade Center, leaving six dead and a thousand wounded. In June 1996, a fuel truck carrying explosives blew up outside the Air Force's Khobar Towers housing facility in Dhahran, Saudi Arabia, killing 19 airmen and injuring 515 others. In 1998, our embassies in Kenya and Tanzania were attacked, the death toll including 13 Americans and nearly 300 foreign nationals. In Aden harbor, in October 2000, a dinghy carrying explosives rammed the side of the USS Cole, killing 17 sailors and wounding 39. When, finally, this phase reached a climax with the second assault on the World Trade Center, on 11 September 2001, a president whose strengths did not include a deep understanding of modern history said the attack had "changed everything."

Some things change; some do not. Contemporary conflict of all kinds springs from the same ancient sources: cultural collision, territorial ambition, economic despair, religious fervor, political miscalculation. But the various modes of warfare differ markedly. By and large, my generation of military professionals trained for and thought about what one might call Type A war—modern war, featuring the clash of mechanized forces fielded by industrial states. We got quite good at this kind of war, but the main idea is pretty simple: the side with air superiority wins, a situation that, for now and maybe only temporarily, plays to our strengths.

Terrorists fight a different kind of war, a Type B war that is in some of its essentials postmodern and, like postmodernism itself, may not represent a coherent set of ideas. The context is an international setting in which power increasingly diffuses to individuals, gangs, corporations, and other nonstate actors, producing both a different sort of violence and a different sort of enemy. The violence can be very painful indeed but must be produced at relatively low cost because the Type B enemy will have little in the way of a treasury. In fact, he'll probably have nothing to lose—no territory to protect, few important targets at risk, perhaps even no life worth living. We therefore cannot expect to deter, but will have to fight this enemy. And we will be unable to entice him to join us in battle since, to be successful, he must pick the time and place. In a way, even the mission, the very purpose for which we fight, must be different. Type A war presents the comparatively simple task of destroying the enemy. In Type B war we take on the much more complicated job of defeating him.

★

We briefly considered bulldozing the headquarters building and putting up a new one in its place—probably the less expensive option—but decided doing so would give the terrorists a public-relations coup. Instead, we patched it up, asking for and getting NATO infrastructure funds for what turned out to be a major reconstruction. Gabriel turned project supervision over to me, and I got to exercise my talent for redecoration. He also decided, while I was fixing up the building, maybe I should look at our whole anti-terrorism posture.

I started a program to make simple security improvements, with emphasis on protecting general officers, the most obvious target. We worked out a redesign of the old occupation-force license plates so they looked more like German tags, making our vehicles less identifiable. In senior-officer housing, we reinforced doors, added external lighting, and created redoubts by hardening bathrooms and installing phones in them. I asked all general officers to take down signs outside their quarters that identified the occupant by name and rank. Our intelligence officer, Brig. Gen. Lenny Perroots (later a lieutenant general and director of the Defense Intelligence Agency) was traveling when the signs came down. On return, his was the only house retaining its general-officer identity. Lenny, who could keep a crowd doubled over in laughter, retold the story at hilarious length.

The Air Force's counterintelligence outfit, the OSI, decided to spend some of its budget on antiterrorist driver training for generals and asked me to do a trial run. It sounded like fun, so I flew to West Virginia for a three-day school run by a former NASCAR race driver. The idea was to avoid entirely or, if that wasn't possible, break through roadblocks, then win the high-speed chase that followed. Backing away from roadblocks required mastery of various quick reversals, like the "J" and "bootleg" turns. Crashing through a barrier also required technique, new stuff for me. The high-speed chase was not so novel, being more like my normal driving. When rain slicked the track just before the nighttime, lights-out exercise, I wrecked a car and upset my instructor. But a little damage was figured into the cost of attendance, and I gave a thumbs-up for the OSI to expand the training opportunity to other general officers.

I had a two-star colleague over at Heidelberg, the chief of staff of US Army Europe. As it happened, he and I spent Thanksgiving in Berlin hosting a dinner for our Russian counterpart from the Group of Soviet Forces, Germany. By tradition, the US and Russian commanders of respective German zones had Thanksgiving dinner at Potsdam, but following the Soviet invasion of Afghanistan, we had downgraded representation to chief-of-staff level. Our Russian counterpart outranked us, as we discovered on the evening of the dinner. He was an army three-star, older, a wide-body model, with a wife to match.

Military attachés assigned to Germany from NATO and Warsaw Pact countries also attended. Just then, the Poles were kicking up a fuss, the thrust provided by Lech Walesa and his shipyard workers from Gdansk. The Polish attaché, an air force colonel, drew me aside, asking whether the United States might be ready to come to the aid of the Poles. He spoke perfect English, so there was no chance of mistaking his meaning. He remembered past East European uprisings, so his heart wasn't in it. But he asked anyway. I told him not to count on us. I, too, recalled how in 1956 we'd fanned Hungarian passions we had no intention of satisfying. I added a caution against making the Russians look bad. He told me not to worry. The Poles were helpless to do anything serious. "The Russians don't give us even a full tank of gas for our armored vehicles."[9]

A general of the MVD (Ministry of Internal Affairs, a sort of secret police), a mean-looking guy with metal teeth, accompanied the Russian three-star. At a certain point, he ostentatiously reached over, lifted the place card from in front of my dinner plate, read it carefully, and stuck it in his pocket. I returned the favor, hitting him with my best fighter-pilot, death-ray stare.

I brought back some solid intelligence: the Russian three-star wasn't crazy about turkey—or pumpkin pie, for that matter.

★

I accompanied Charlie Gabriel to Naples, where a four-star admiral, Bill Crowe, commanded NATO's Southern Region and served concurrently as the senior US Navy officer in Europe. This was my

---

9 Within a month of this Thanksgiving evening, the Russians stage-managed a crackdown on Walesa. The Poles declared martial law and rounded up many of his Solidarity Party supporters.

first meeting with Crowe, who would become our joint commander in the Pacific and then serve with distinction as chairman of the Joint Chiefs of Staff. Following his retirement, he would endorse the presidential candidacy of Bill Clinton, who rewarded him with the post of ambassador to the Court of St. James.

Crowe took our party out to the Isle of Capri in his "barge." A bit of an egghead (PhD, Princeton) and therefore someone the Navy was not quite sure about, Crowe was nevertheless a man of large scope and considerable charm.

In June 1982, just under nine years since the Yom Kippur disaster, Israel's air force got even. Using all sorts of electronic warfare gadgetry, it thoroughly confused the elaborate and supposedly capable SAM network set up by Syria in Lebanon's Bekaa Valley, then put it out of action with antiradar missiles and cluster bombs. When the Syrian Air Force rose to the bait, the Israelis essentially destroyed it in air-to-air engagements. Syria lost 80 MiG-21s and MiG-23s, and Israel none of its F-15s or F-16s, in what must be the most one-sided dogfight in history.

Unhappily, the Israelis subsequently got bogged down on the ground in Lebanon. Beirut came under siege, there were massacres in the Palestinian refugee camps at Sabra and Shatila, and southern Lebanon endured a long occupation that did nobody any good.

In a great development, Charlie Gabriel became chief of staff when Gen. Lew Allen retired in the summer of 1982. It had been a while since an overseas commander had risen to become our chief. In addition, we hadn't had a real fighter pilot in charge of the Air Force since Tooey Spaatz, who in any case switched to big airplanes after World War I. At the Ramstein headquarters at least, Charlie was "our" general, so we felt like we were part of his success.

We saw Gabriel off in grand style, with the usual round of banquets, speeches, going-away gifts. The Germans, with whom Charlie had been enormously popular, did us one better, holding a torchlight ceremony at the soccer stadium in the nearby town of Kaiserslautern. Actually, kind of creepy. At best it was Lohengrin crossing the Rhine; at worst you got that old *Kristallnacht* feeling.

Shortly after the arrival of Gabriel's replacement, I was told of my reassignment to Headquarters Tactical Air Command, at Langley AFB, Virginia. I returned from Europe, having spent seven years there in five different jobs and three different countries.

Chapter 10

Langley

*At the very heart of warfare lies doctrine. It represents the
central beliefs for waging war in order to achieve victory.*
—Curtis LeMay

As a colonel and operations deputy of the 37th Fighter Wing,
Wilbur L. "Bill" Creech had been my boss at Phu Cat. When Phu
Cat converted from F-100s to F-4s, I relocated with Misty to Tuy
Hoa, and Creech went to Saigon to work for Dave Jones, a rising
star who went on to become Air Force chief of staff, then chairman
of the joint chiefs. Jones liked Creech and subsequently provided
powerful sponsorship. By May 1978, Creech was installed at Langley as commander of Tactical Air Command. Years later, Charlie
Gabriel told me Creech had offered "three good colonels" in trade to
bring me back from Europe to be a wing commander in TAC. Charlie had turned him down. But now, installed at the Pentagon as our
new chief, Gabriel agreed to farm me out to Creech.

Bill Creech was a tester, and ruthless with officers who did
not meet the test. Picking up and discarding with velocity, he
built around him a cadre of very capable men. He had two vice-
commanders while I was at Langley—Pete Piotrowski, who got a

fourth star as vice chief of staff and ended up running NORAD and Space Command, and Bob Russ, who followed soon after Creech as TAC's commander. Creech's deputy for operations, Bob Reed, became a four-star as chief of staff at NATO's senior military headquarters, SHAPE. Creech's exec, Joe Ralston, was an especially gifted officer who went on to be JCS vice-chairman and the first blue-suit SACEUR since Larry Norstad. Johnny Jumper, Creech's aide, would be the Air Force's 17th chief of staff. In brief, Creech formed and shaped a cohort that would have extraordinary influence inside the Air Force and on the nation's defenses for years after he retired.

Two other officers had a Creech association but were slightly different cases. Larry Welch spent many years at Langley, both on the TAC staff and as commander of the 1st Wing, stationed there and equipped with F-15s. He served time as Creech's deputy for plans and his deputy for operations, but (like me) couldn't really be considered a Creech guy. (My promotion to BG came while serving under Charlie Gabriel, and follow-on service as his chief of staff in Europe labeled me a Gabriel guy.) Larry Welch had enjoyed major-league sponsorship from Creech's predecessor, Bob Dixon, but the fan club reached well beyond Dixon and Creech. As Dixon famously observed, Welch could throw Jell-O at the wall and make it stick. Everybody had the highest regard for Larry. Super smart and absolutely incorruptible, Welch went on to earn top marks from Gabriel as vice chief, served briefly as commander of Strategic Air Command, then returned to Washington to succeed Charlie as chief of staff.

The other officer, Mike Dugan, was with me at Langley as Creech's inspector general and later as TAC's deputy for operations. Of course, Mike and I went back a long ways and had watched each other's progress. Though junior to me in the old days, he'd beaten me to colonel and therefore ranked just ahead of me on the BG list of 1981. (He was number 20, and I, 21, of 58 colonels selected.) For some reason, Creech was not quite so high on Mike. On the other hand, after I recovered from the new-guy treatment, Creech pushed my early promotion to two-star and slowed Dugan down a bit, so that I jumped a year ahead of Mike in relative rank.

★

On 18 January 1982, while I was still in Europe, all four aircraft of the Thunderbird Diamond flew into the ground at the bottom of a line-abreast loop. Apparently, during a training session at Indian Springs, lead experienced some sort of flight-control problem, and the wingmen followed him in. Devastated, Bill Creech stood the team down and thought seriously about quitting the air show business. He shut himself in his office and ran the tape of the crash over and over.

The entire Air Force held its breath. No one wanted to take the decision away from Creech. Not only did he run the major command to which the Thunderbirds were assigned, Creech himself was a former team member and was widely regarded as knowing a lot about the air show business. Nevertheless, the team belonged to the whole Air Force, everybody understood its representational and recruiting value, and no one wanted to quit. Charlie Gabriel was prepared to intervene if needed to keep the team going, but at length, and to the great relief of all concerned, Creech came to the right decision: the team would start up again for the 1983 show season. He also decided the Thunderbirds would transition out of the T-38 and into the F-16, an excellent move bringing the team back into a combat aircraft.

I arrived at TAC Headquarters in the fall of 1982, after the major decisions had been made and during a time when Creech was spending a big part of every day supervising the final phases of Thunderbird reorganization. Your basic poster child for tenacity, Creech took on the team as a project, micromanaging every detail and getting a lot of it right. I got a pass on most of this since I was late to the party. I was also the new guy, Creech taking about six months to decide I was not a complete idiot. In any case, I was happy to be left out. Creech worked through Bob Reed, the

*"Take This Job
and Shove It,"
People's Fest,
Zaragoza Air Base,
Spain, 1978.*

*1980, commander, 20th Fighter Wing,
RAF Upper Heyford, United Kingdom.*

The 20th Fighter Wing senior wives, 1981.

RAF Upper Heyford, UK, planting trees to hide camouflaged aircraft shelters.

1981, breakfast with Chief of Staff Lew Allen.

Ellie and I after I was "wetted down," following my last F-111 flight.

Charlie Gabriel and Ellie pin on my first star.

Thanksgiving at Potsdam, November 1981.
The Russian guy has metal teeth.

operations deputy, and the commander at Nellis, both guys getting phone calls in the middle of the night.

The hazing I took during initiation at TAC was not lightened by my performance when given a small taste of the Thunderbird restart issue. Within a few weeks of arriving at Langley and still coming up to speed on my new job, Creech asked me to look at the draft of a manual describing the team's future operating procedures. I said, "OK, I'm scheduled for a couple days' Christmas leave in California. Can I read it over the holiday?" He said fine, maybe a little disappointed I didn't cancel Christmas. I soon realized he'd be really upset if he were not already quite pleased with the manual, which had been through several iterations and now contained content mostly of his own authorship.

Sitting in California's gentle December sun, I went through the manual carefully. Before leaving the team in 1968, I'd written what I thought was a pretty good book on how to do solo work, sage advice either lost or purposely discarded. Certainly, nothing of mine survived into the pages Creech had asked me to review. Not wishing to mark up the document, I penciled observations and recommendations on slips of paper and clipped these to appropriate pages. There were many such bits of paper.

Back at Langley following the holiday, I sent the manual across the street to the front office. Immediately, my hotline broke its silence, the initial use of a direct connection to Creech I didn't know I had. I scrambled to find the source of the ringing, the instrument hidden in a drawer. Could I come over?

Ushered in, I saw Creech with the manual open in front of him. He started with my first note. We discussed the point I had raised, he judged me wrong, wadded up the small slip of paper and tossed it into his wastebasket. We moved on to the next dumb idea. After about 50 such rejections, he decided maybe I'd had a point in one of those earlier recommendations, pawed through the trash, and fished it out. But that was it. I was batting one for 50, an average that had better improve.

The 1982 Thunderbird accident changed the air show for good. Creech's detailed, hands-on supervision had the effect of simplifying maneuvers, raising altitudes and regularizing (as well as much improving) training. The team got increased manpower and other support, and the show schedule was cut back. Creech's special relationship with the team continued to his last day in uniform—and beyond, since he retired to Las Vegas, becoming an on-scene, active ingredient.

In perhaps his greatest act of statesmanship relating to the team, Creech destroyed all but a single videotape of the Diamond accident, then snipped off the final few frames showing actual ground impact. In response to media requests, the Air Force eventually released the altered tape, but the nation was spared having to watch this episode over and over again.

My duties as Creech's deputy for plans were interesting, if a distant second in order of importance to those of the deputy for operations. TAC was mostly an administrative rather than a war-fighting command, so its focus was inward, on its major subordinates— First, Ninth, and Twelfth Air Forces, each of which did have joint war-fighting responsibilities—and on the combat crew training workload at Nellis, Luke, and Tyndall. First Air Force's role as a component of NORAD made it the workhorse of North American air defense. Ninth Air Force, our component of US Central Command, was an old formation, notable for its performance over the Normandy beaches and onward into central Europe in World War II. (It would soon become even more famous when it performed impressively during Desert Storm.) Twelfth Air Force, TAC's component of US Southern Command, was another fine old outfit with an important history and responsibilities in Central and South America, including for the so-called War on Drugs. Thus, while I did very little actual war planning as TAC's "planner," I held a watching brief on documents prepared by the joint commands in charge of the Middle East, Latin America, and the air defense of

North America. A small section working for me reviewed the contingency planning done by each of these combatant commands.

For conflict in Europe or the Pacific, TAC's job was to augment forces already in place. Both European and Pacific commands drew up elaborate reinforcement plans, and the Joint Staff lined up stateside units for deployment. On call, these formations would move to the theater. A schedule for doing this—known as a time-phased force deployment list, or TPFDL (pronounced "tipfiddle")—established the order in which units moved and identified their destinations. This turned out to be a complicated business, with lots of moving parts, as well as an element of gaming. Much prestige accrued to those needed quickly, and a place high on the TPFDL had budget implications, early responders being favored for training and readiness dollars.

If producing plans for large-scale reinforcement was complex, executing them was out of the question. Helmuth von Moltke the Elder, himself no slouch as a planner, famously observed that no plan survives contact with the enemy. Certainly, no major reinforcement ever goes as scheduled. Count on it: the first day's activities will not follow the playbook; changes will carom into the lineup for each succeeding day; very shortly, nothing will remain of the original scheme. Nevertheless, thinking this a perfect problem for computers, the JCS established the Joint Deployment Agency in 1979 and charged it with producing Newtonian plans for clockwork reinforcement. The JDA worked long, hard, and without success. During my time at TAC, reinforcement planning needed to improve markedly to achieve the status of a major disappointment. TPFDLs were notional, game plans suitable for about the first five minutes of any actual crisis. After that, we'd improvise, draw plays in the huddle. If the opposition cut us some slack (as would happen in Desert Shield) we'd eventually get the pieces in place and straighten the lines a bit, but even this modest accomplishment would demand superhuman, hands-on management in real time.

The only consolation: Air Force reinforcement planning was in much better shape than that of the other services, so we were not the pacing factor in cleaning up the mess.

Beyond its war-planning responsibilities, TAC's plans shop was a grab bag of disparate functions. I had a division that was supposed to play a large role in the acquisition of new equipment by writing "concepts." In an effort to rein in service appetites, the Defense Department had a rule that equipment requirements must rest on a concept, an elaborate description of how the new gear will be used. The idea seemed to be that we should sit around and dream up questions, like, "What would I do with an invisible airplane, if I had one?" After writing down the answer, we could use this "concept paper" as the basis for working up a hardware requirement and, if all went well, in a decade or two, we'd have stealth.

Sometimes the system works this way, but it's usually the other way round. Roosevelt did not write Einstein a note suggesting we could avoid a million casualties invading Japan if he would just get moving on this chain-reaction thing. Time after time, the technology comes forward before we have a good idea how to use it. Nevertheless, regs are regs, so my Concepts Division worked closely with TAC's deputy for requirements, making sure that any demand for new equipment rested on a supporting concept statement.

Working with TAC requirements brought me in contact with Mike Loh, then a colonel but a future four-star. He was extra smart, especially important at this point because we were beginning work on the requirement for an F-15 follow-on air-superiority aircraft, an airplane we were calling the advanced tactical fighter. (At length, this would turn out to be the Lockheed F-22, the first squadron of which entered service in December 2005, 24 years after we laid down the requirement.) In my view, this was our most critical new-equipment need; we had to get it right. When I arrived at Langley in the fall of 1982, Loh and his people were already hammering out operating characteristics of such an aircraft—stealth, supersonic cruise speed without afterburner, and avionics integration being the most important ones—and my staff was drafting the concept paper and establishing a force-structure target for 750 of these new aircraft.

Another of my responsibilities involved programming. Annually, the secretary of defense gave the services a future funding profile called the Five-Year Defense Program (FYDP), a revenue "topline" going out five years beyond the current budget year. The services responded with a program objective memorandum, or POM, a detailed proposal for how to spend the money. Following submission of the individual service POMs, DOD competed one against the other, moving money around to fund what it regarded the most meritorious programs. So plenty was at stake for the services in the annual POM drill.

The same sort of contest for out-year funding occurred inside the Air Force. Tactical programs jockeyed for position with strategic, mobility, or space programs, all having powerful, four-star sponsorship. Functions that cut across mission lines, like intelligence, medical care, security, or communications, scrambled for funding. This competition, a survival of the fittest programs, should produce the best defense posture for the country, and pretty well did; though, as with biological evolution, humans—DOD, the White House, industry, Congress—contaminated natural processes.

Literally hundreds of tactical programs existed, each with detailed cost and manpower elements, and all changing all the time. Just keeping track of the database was a full-time job, but it was in juggling priorities and fending off competing programs that sharp elbows were needed.

My programming responsibilities gave me a good seat from which to follow the jousting inside the Air Force and among the services for budget dollars. The two-and-a-half years I spent at Langley, from fall 1982 until spring 1985, were the heart of the Reagan Administration's defense buildup. Things would never be better for us, yet the poor-mouthing did not abate. Creech joined in, making speeches and giving interviews in which he claimed the correct benchmark for defense spending was 7 percent of GDP.

I had no idea where he came up with this number, except it was more than we were getting.

I suppose it's understandable, but I found it painful to watch.

Virginia sends several fingers of land southeast into Chesapeake Bay, but only the one bounded by the James and York Rivers and terminating at Hampton is called the Virginia Peninsula. The rivers give names to Jamestown, America's first settlement, and Yorktown, site of the battle that effectively ended the Revolutionary War. Williamsburg, an early capital of Virginia Colony, occupies high ground in the middle of the peninsula. The country's oldest military base then still in use, Fort Monroe, stands at the tip, near Hampton Township at Old Point Comfort. It was the largest stone fort ever built by the Army and the only one inside a moat. Robert E. Lee was stationed there as a lieutenant, Edgar Allan Poe as a sergeant major of artillery. At the start of the Civil War, Lincoln rushed reinforcements to Fort Monroe, so it remained in Union hands throughout the conflict. It was safe enough the president could visit the place in May of 1862, two months after the ironclads Merrimack and Monitor fought to a draw at Hampton Roads and three weeks before Lee took over the Army of Northern Virginia. After the war, Jefferson Davis was imprisoned for two years in one of the fort's open, unheated casemates—treatment perhaps meant to be lethal.

Thus, the peninsula smells of history and so does Langley Field. In 1916, though we had no notion we might want air bases for national defense, the Army figured its embryonic air arm needed a place where it could do research, as well as experiment with and try out airplanes. The aviation pioneer Samuel Pierpont Langley had avoided fatal accidents by catapulting aircraft into the Potomac. Thinking this a good approach, the Army found a flat spot near open water north of Hampton and made it the first land ever purchased by our government for purposes relating to aviation. The 35 buildings constructed at Langley between 1917 and 1920 constitute the largest and most historic group of permanent structures associated with early aviation history, including the oldest aircraft hangar. The National Advisory Committee for Aeronautics (NACA) was also an early settler, opening Langley Aeronautical Laboratory, the nation's earliest civilian aeronautical-research institution. In 1920, NACA built the first of what would become 40 or so wind tunnels and for the next three decades did the world's most important aeronautical research, producing a heroic period of aircraft design.[10]

Ellie and I lived on base, in one of the large Tudor revival homes that lined the right bank of the Back River, a tributary of the York. The house was a bit large for us, with Mark now a Peace Corps volunteer in Ecuador and Brian starting undergraduate studies at Cal Berkeley, so we rattled around the place. There was a dinette just off the kitchen with windows looking into the back of a medium-sized, dense scrub. A pair of cardinals nested there in spring, and we watched as if at a natural-history exhibit. The cardinals fetched ribs and stringers for a sturdy nest, lined it with grass, bits of paper, fine hair. The female incubated three eggs for 10 days or so, the male making home deliveries. Punctual, upstanding parents, they took turns feeding the young for another 10 days. Two of the chicks were up and out of the nest in due course, but the third had something wrong on one side—maybe an injury— and couldn't learn to fly quickly. It hopped around under the bush for a couple of days, chipping loudly, seemingly doomed, an aviator with no talent for foot soldiering. Worried sick, the parents flew top cover, made alarm calls, displayed bravely against any threat. Finally, the youngster struggled into the air, tentative at first, but able, finally, to follow his siblings' pioneering route from scrub to tree to telephone wire.

---

10 The absorption of NACA into NASA in 1958 certainly helped put a man on the moon, but "aeronautics"—the first "A" in NASA—has since tended to get lost in space.

The following spring our cardinals were displaced by fascist robins who expropriated the nest. Too big for it, they bulged out the sides, and also treated their chicks indifferently, a disappointing contrast to the diligent cardinals.

Our yard ran down to the Back River. Mallards came up and made a parade ground of the lawn. Ellie left a Pyrex dish outside with water in it, and a mother duck improvised a wading pool for her large brood. Pecan trees yielded sacks of nuts I shelled at day's end, an eye on the evening news. We took walks along the river. Wind tunnels loomed all around—large, air-breathing creatures that gave the place a science fiction feel. I walked to work in good weather, something I'd been able to do in no other Air Force job.

☆

Creech was the best-ever manipulator of the Air Force's operations and maintenance (O&M) budget. As was the practice at all major commands, he withheld a fraction of annual flying program dollars to cover contingencies. He then had his wing commanders vie for the reserved money, mostly in the form of facility-upgrade requests. Moreover—and this was the key—he reinforced success. Maybe a base already had the best facilities in the Free World, but if the commander showed he could spend money well, Creech gave him more. This was, of course, a way for the rich to get richer, but it evened out because if the commander at a run-down base wasn't smart enough to know how to fix it, Creech not only stopped the flow of money, he got himself a new commander. In addition, Creech established TAC standards for things like facility design and base master planning, including detailed guidance on such matters as paint selection, curbing, landscaping, and so forth. During his five-plus years at the helm, TAC blossomed, becoming the envy of the rest of the Air Force, and even the other services. Everyone wanted to know how he did it.

After I was properly TACemsized, Creech began to share confidences. One day, chuckling, he told me that in Omaha the SAC commander, Gen. Bennie Davis, had hired a consulting firm for a million dollars or so to figure out how SAC could duplicate TAC's success. Creech wished aloud he had the million dollars to put on facility projects.

Joe Ralston stopped by one afternoon to brief me on the F-117. The stealth program had been under way for a decade—the initial fighter squadron already operational—but this was the first I'd heard of it. Amazing. I hadn't credited us with the ability to keep a secret. Better yet, we continued to maintain reasonably tight security on the program for some years to come, even though we were flying more than 1,000 people daily back and forth from Nellis to the bed-down site.

Creech sent me to visit the operating location, a secret base where Creech had spent a lot of money without much oversight. It was a beautiful setup, and Creech would end up getting in hot water for gold plating. On my return to Langley, he asked my impressions. Of course, I liked what he'd done. Questioned about the aircraft itself, I said it looked a little ungainly, but that was OK since, basically, it was a night, straight-and-level bomber. He thought it was beautiful and said so, once again highlighting my poor judgment. I nodded, though the thing would always remind me of a cockroach.

We rightly regard the F-117 as a fourth-generation jet fighter, but only because of its stealth. In every other performance aspect, it was inferior to the F-16. Nevertheless, here was another revolutionary development in warfare. We fight at a distance, the jab our punch of choice. The advent of guided munitions meant this blow would nearly always land flush on the chin. Now precision was mated to stealth, meaning the other guy couldn't see it coming, couldn't cover up.

Stealth is the way to take down integrated air defenses. There is also an electronic warfare dimension to the job, but dedicated

EW jammers like the Navy's EA-6 or our own EF-111 are very costly to buy and keep up to date. In addition, you take a very capable airplane out of the fight and commit it to support. And, as it happens, the Air Force does not exist for the purpose of not getting shot down.

In the future, electronic warfare capabilities will be integral to combat aircraft, to the extent they are needed. Stealth is the sunrise, EW the sunset, part of defeating air defenses.

Thus, precision changed everything. Stealth changed the rest.

As we entered World War I, the Army found a military mission for what had started as a research site at Langley Field, putting in combat aircraft and transferring experimental work to Dayton, Ohio. In 1921, airplanes operating out of here sent the German dreadnought Ostfriesland to the bottom in 21.5 minutes. The Navy, hoping to show battleships unsinkable, set unrealistic rules for the exercise, so Billy Mitchell got in a little trouble for using 2,000-pound bombs. He nevertheless celebrated by throwing a party at the Langley Officers Club.

Langley was also the first center of professional education for airmen. After its establishment at Langley, the Air Service Tactical School produced a manual titled *Fundamental Doctrine of the Air Service* that pretty much mimicked the party line: success in combat depended entirely on infantry; air operations made sense only as an adjunct to the ground battle.

The Tactical School relocated to Maxwell Field, Alabama, in 1931, but in some ways Langley remained at the center of Air Force concerns about doctrine. One of my duties as deputy for plans was to work the doctrine issue, especially the so-called TAC-TRADOC dialogue, a forum for ironing out differences in the competing worldviews of the Air Force and Army.

Just what is doctrine? Curt LeMay thought it "at the very heart of warfare."[11] If so, what is the distinction between doctrine and principles of war or, for that matter, doctrine and tactics? I thought I had a pretty good grasp of tactics, the moves that actually work in small-unit engagements, and I believed I understood the principles of war, guiding axioms for positioning and maneuvering larger formations. As for anything else, like most airmen, I held fast to a few key beliefs: in modern, industrial war, forces at the earth's surface have almost no chance of success if they must breathe hostile air; if used properly, airpower can achieve important, even decisive results; in a theater of operations, only someone who knows the business should direct air operations, including especially the important matter of selecting targets. Thus, a handful of ideas, more or less timeless and therefore not in need of careful and continuous revision, constituted my idea of doctrine.

I suppose I never acquired a good understanding of doctrine, including the question of why people got so fired up about it. Anyway, whatever doctrine was, the commanders at TAC and TRADOC engaged in a "dialogue" about it, a series of meetings and staff discussions aimed at bridging service differences. It was my job to prepare Creech for this dialogue. When I arrived at Langley, Creech's partner in the conversation was Glenn Otis, a great Army officer.

The Army's Training and Doctrine Command (TRADOC) was located at Fort Monroe, a few miles down the road from Langley. Both TAC and TRADOC were four-star headquarters, but in other ways a mismatch. An operating command charged with

---

11 In this matter I found myself (yet again) out of sync with LeMay's thinking, as I understood it. LeMay was a bull—strong, aggressive, fearless—and he built an air force in his own image. I thought we needed a different sort of air force, one more like the toreador than the bull.

maintaining the readiness of most of the Air Force's theater war-fighting capacity, TAC in addition developed doctrine for use by tactical forces—an important responsibility but necessarily secondary to the readiness job. I had a doctrine shop, with half a dozen people assigned.

By contrast, TRADOC—a more-or-less pure training and education command—had no operational role. Heading its Doctrine Division was Maj. Gen. Don Morelli, a fine officer whose untimely death was a great loss to the Army and the country. Ill but still at work, he had maybe 50 people at Fort Monroe, but even this large resource vastly understated the Army's investment in doctrine. Every Army branch—infantry, armor, artillery, and so forth—had its own school that, among other things, developed doctrine. Sitting atop this elaborate network of doctrine authors and guarding the gate to the inner temple was the Command and General Staff College at Fort Leavenworth. Thus, the Army put much time and talent into doctrine and published significant changes as frequently as thought necessary, which to an outsider seemed pretty often. That TRADOC, a major command, included "Doctrine" in its name shows how important the matter was to the Army.[12]

Reduced to essentials, the doctrine debate between TAC and TRA-DOC was about *who* would decide how airpower was to be used. But underlying this question was a more fundamental unresolved issue: what is the proper objective of military action? You would

---

12 All services publish documents that look a bit like doctrine but are more akin to marketing materials. Since my entire focus at Langley was on the TAC-TRADOC dialogue, I omit any discussion here of the Navy and Marine Corps, but we should acknowledge they are very good at the game. When he was secretary of the Navy, John Lehman produced an extended advertisement called *The Maritime Strategy*, which argued that 80 percent of the Earth is covered by water, that most of the world's population is settled within a few kilometers of the beach, and that all this territory could be controlled by the US Navy, if only it had 600 ships.

think this a rather important question, and the debate about it should be high-minded and serious, but at the most senior levels, the issue was often simply not joined, there being no wish on either side to dissolve the comity of the relationship. Where the debate did occur, in the engine room, it usually spiraled into a shouting match about which form of military power was the more important.[13]

If, with Clausewitz, you believed the proper target is the *enemy army* and submission of the *opposing ground force* is the only outcome of armed conflict that can be regarded as successful, then the Army had a fair—though only a fair—argument for primacy.[14] Accepting this premise and building on it, the Army saw air forces as a powerful auxiliary, a deliverer of critical support. They relied on Air Force transport to get to the fight. They wanted air reconnaissance to increase their understanding of the battlefield situation. They had a considerable liking for close air support (CAS), which they saw as a kind of flying artillery. The Army seemed to want a relationship much like the one the Marines had created, an air-land team in which the Air Force acts as the Army's air arm. Thus, while they argued it could not be decisive, they regarded air support as of such importance they did not want decisions about how to use it left to the Air Force.

Unhappily, the early airpower enthusiasts—the Italian Giulio Douhet, our own Billy Mitchell, others—turned this entire chain of thought on its head, arguing that land armies were more-or-less

---

13 This attitude is seldom seen on the battlefield, where every kind of help is welcome. It's in the rarefied air of the Pentagon, or at other large, tranquil headquarters that this question arises, because how you answer it has a direct impact on budgets and end strength.

14 Many in the Army went further, *defining* victory as closure with and defeat of the enemy's ground force. Any other outcome, even one favoring our country, was *by definition* something other than victory. Such claims stand in interesting contrast with, for instance, Sun Tzu's view of the army as an instrument for delivering the *coup de grâce* to an enemy previously made vulnerable.

irrelevant because they could be flown around and over, bypassed in making direct, conclusive strikes at the enemy's heartland. In my opinion, these gentlemen overstated the case, and because they did there has been, since the mid-1920s, an ongoing, sometimes quite nasty, always unproductive argument about whether, in fact, airpower *is* decisive in this way. To say the least, soldiers have been skeptical. As evidence for their view, they cite the report of the Strategic Bombing Survey of World War II, which established that bombing had much less impact on Germany's economy than we supposed and, further, the inconclusive results obtained by airpower in both Korea and Vietnam.[15]

The idea that, on its own, airpower can *never* be decisive has seeped into the groundwater of Army thought, a belief so persistent it has become a kind of physical constant, like the mass of the proton. The Army view is quite understandable. If "boots on the battlefield" constitutes not only the definitive measure of victory but also the indispensable precondition for achieving it, then we need to fund the Army first and best, which is what most countries do.

Dialogue is a waste of time unless we agree on definitions, so we should start with the matter of what victory actually means. Army officers have tended to think in absolutist terms. Grant defined victory as the enemy's "unconditional surrender," though he allowed healing conditions at Appomattox and elsewhere. MacArthur claimed, "In war there is no substitute for victory," the sort of cheerleading that moves the crowd but not the football. Clearly, our fascination with unqualified, total victory was not helpful in the termination phases of the Second World War. Roosevelt's stated goal of "unconditional surrender," in which Churchill reluctantly acquiesced, stiffened German resistance and reduced the likelihood

---

15 The atomic attacks that ended Japanese resistance and avoided a costly invasion of the Home Islands are regarded as the exception that proves the rule. Concerning the forms of conflict that remain plausible, nuclear weaponry seems for the moment essentially unusable.

of effective internal opposition to Hitler. In the Pacific, we in the end acceded to Japan's holdout condition, that the emperor remain as a symbol of sovereignty. There is much evidence that, had we been willing to show this flexibility earlier, we might have avoided the incineration of Hiroshima and Nagasaki.

In fact, "victory," like the "national interest," is an increasingly mushy concept. Armed conflict seldom ends in an unmixed, binary result. Generally, the needle comes to rest somewhere in a spectrum of outcomes yielding greater or lesser advantage to one of the sides. It may be better to think that all military forces, ground, sea, and air, exist for the purpose of achieving, in combination with the other instruments of national power, specific policy objectives stated by the political leadership. The side that more or less achieves its objectives can claim victory.

Moreover, even if victory's sole meaning is the destruction of hostile ground forces, airpower, acting independently, is quite competent to the task. Of course, armies can be defeated by riflemen firing at close range, and also by being battered, by being cold, by being hungry, by losing hope. It's obvious that all these effects can be achieved from the air.

In judging this matter, we should be careful not to be blinded by atmospherics. Soldiers usually figure prominently in peace ceremonies. It may be a sword or sidearm that is handed across the table. Thus, victory is decorated with the symbols of land warfare, an agreeable tradition and perhaps even important in the process of normalizing relations between the contending parties. But we should not confuse victory's essence with its trappings.

In the end, the issue between TAC and TRADOC was this: who decides how airpower will be used? The contemporaneous Army doctrine, called AirLand Battle, had been adopted in 1982, about the time I showed up at Langley. This document addressed the responsibilities of the corps commander, a three-star general at the head of an organization of two or more Army divisions, altogether maybe 40,000 to 60,000 soldiers. AirLand Battle doctrine claimed the corps commander must control events in front of him to a depth that depended on the speed ground forces were moving, but perhaps as far as 300 kilometers beyond the line of contact with the enemy, in normal circumstances. In this extended region, the Army, by doctrinal fiat, made the corps commander responsible for "synchronizing" fires.

The Air Force has always been content to hand authority for close air support over to the Army. When operating close to friendly troops, we do nothing without the Army's blessing, usually in the form of direction by a forward air controller in constant contact with forces on the ground. Some ambiguity attaches as to where close air support ends and another of airpower's roles—what we call interdiction—begins, but to a first approximation, we can say the phase transition occurs at the fire support coordination line (FSCL). This is a battlefield control measure, a line on the map that assigns responsibilities to cooperating commanders. In the case of the FSCL, the line is something like a city limits. Inside, the police (Army) have jurisdiction; outside, it's the county sheriff (Air Force).

The ground commander establishes the FSCL, placing it, one hopes, with the agreement of the air commander. Typically, it lies 30 to 50 kilometers forward of our most advanced ground positions, a distance more than adequate for safety and at the limit of artillery fire that may require coordination with air attack. Best case, the ground and air commanders draw the FSCL along some easily identifiable topographic or cultural feature—a river, a line of hills, a major road—so aircrews have a visual cue when they fly beyond the FSCL and can attack freely, without concern for the safety of friendly forces.

Now along comes this new AirLand Battle doctrine, establishing, *unilaterally*, a requirement for the corps commander, not the overall ground commander—in a theater of operations, likely a four-star in charge of several corps—to synchronize fires, including Air

Force bombing, out to 300 kilometers, and maybe farther.[16] This was a long way from close air support, so AirLand Battle doctrine also invented a new combat role for the Air Force—battlefield air interdiction (BAI)—which we could describe as interdiction under the corps commander's control.

It was a mistake to think that either Bill Creech or I would agree. During the time I worked on the TAC-TRADOC dialogue, we did lots of talking and made almost no progress.

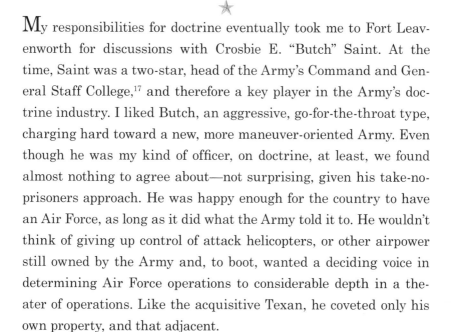

My responsibilities for doctrine eventually took me to Fort Leavenworth for discussions with Crosbie E. "Butch" Saint. At the time, Saint was a two-star, head of the Army's Command and General Staff College,[17] and therefore a key player in the Army's doctrine industry. I liked Butch, an aggressive, go-for-the-throat type, charging hard toward a new, more maneuver-oriented Army. Even though he was my kind of officer, on doctrine, at least, we found almost nothing to agree about—not surprising, given his take-no-prisoners approach. He was happy enough for the country to have an Air Force, as long as it did what the Army told it to. He wouldn't think of giving up control of attack helicopters, or other airpower still owned by the Army and, to boot, wanted a deciding voice in determining Air Force operations to considerable depth in a theater of operations. Like the acquisitive Texan, he coveted only his own property, and that adjacent.

---

16 At the time, of course, "fires" beyond the FSCL originated almost entirely with the Air Force. In this combat zone, the corps commander didn't have much Army firepower to synchronize with what the Air Force was already doing out there. Consequently, the Army launched a series of programs to develop and procure rocket-powered munitions capable of reaching beyond the FSCL. At least initially, such munitions have proved so complex and expensive that the Army can buy them only in small numbers, making possession of these weapons a slender thread on which to hang the corps commander's bid to control the deeper battle.

17 Later, the four-star commander of US Army Europe.

The problem with this approach: air warfare is (literally) a game of three-dimensional chess, with little prospect of easy victory if, on our side of the board, a different player controls the moves at each level. Were it in my power, I'd correct the mistake made after World War II, when airpower was cut up like a pizza so everyone could have a slice.

During my stay at Fort Leavenworth, I was taken to meet the overall commander there, a three-star by the name of Carl Vuono, a nice man ticketed to be a future Army chief of staff. In Vuono's office, I met another visitor to Fort Leavenworth, Colin Powell, like me, still wearing the single star of a brigadier general. But he would soon be promoted to major general, beating me by two months.

Our headquarters' manning document called for me to have a brigadier general as an assistant and, at length, I was issued one of the Air Force's most promising officers to fill that post. I felt lucky to get him. However, the day he arrived at Langley, he was interviewed by and made an unfavorable impression on General Creech, who arranged on the spot to have him reassigned, establishing a new record for general officer job tenure at TAC headquarters. The officer hung around for a couple of days waiting for orders. His household goods arrived and he made the reasonable request that the furniture stay in the van for shipment to his next post. The moving company would have none of it. The stuff was unloaded, spread out on the sidewalk, checked for damage, then reloaded for onward shipment, giving the newly remarried general's wife her first exposure to the ways of the Air Force.

Bill Creech measured every aspect of officers working for him, including personal appearance, where his obsessiveness seemed odd to me. In one exchange, he complained at length about an officer whose untrimmed eyebrows supposedly clouded an other-wise sunny record. (I took this as a not too subtle hint I should cope with my own eyebrows, which tended to be unruly.) Creech insisted that officers perform well and, in addition, saw no reason why they should not look good while doing so. He certainly was fixated on his own physical appearance, and not above a little cosmetic enhancement.

While I did not believe officers had to be ugly or smell bad, I cared about actual performance, and little else. Granted, I thought physical fitness and good hygiene were baseline performance ingredients. But nothing about pushups, or brushing your teeth, is contrived. It's recourse to the artificial—hair dye or the plastic surgeon's snip and tuck—that seems effete, that contributes nothing to combat readiness.

I got to fly only a little at Langley, adding a few hours of T-39 time when I used that airplane for official travel. While there, I passed 25 years of service, the cutoff date for receiving incentive pay, whether you fly or not. Or rather, as Billy Boles, TAC's first-rate personnel chief, assured me, I would continue to get flight pay, but at the zero rate.

Regarding doctrine, the key questions for the Air Force are: What are we trying to accomplish in war? What is the role of airpower in getting it done? If the question of how to use airpower is contested, who makes the decision? For what it's worth, here are my views on these three questions: What the country accepts as a successful outcome in war—what we define as victory—is a political, not a military question, and therefore not a doctrinal matter. How important a role does airpower play? Whether it's decisive or not—a controversial question, with the recent evidence running against the Army—it is of at least equal importance, the reason each of the other services, including the Army, has at great expense kept a lot of its own airpower and seeks to retain control of it. Finally, the joint commander is the boss, not the ground commander or any of potentially several corps commanders who may report to the ground commander. In making decisions about how airpower will be employed, the joint commander would do well to listen to his senior airman.

On balance, my work in the doctrine vineyards left me a little dispirited. Too much of what passed for doctrine was untestable and therefore of no scientific content. Dogma pretended to be data; faith paraded as fact; evidence-immune assertions were arbitrarily promoted to axioms. In the discussion, what seemed to matter was how many people lined up on each side of an issue and how intensely each side held its opinions—a procedure for defining politics, not the military art.

After two-and-a-half years at TAC headquarters, I was promoted to lieutenant general and sent to the Pentagon. Maj. Gen. Chuck Horner replaced me as the deputy for plans at TAC.

Chapter 11

Air Staff

The most difficult and most important decisions in respect to objectives are not what to do. They are, first, what to abandon as no longer worthwhile and, second, what to give priority to and what to concentrate on.
—Peter Drucker, *The Age of Discontinuity*

When I returned to the Pentagon in May 1985, the deputy chief of staff for programs and resources (DCS/PR) had three main duties. First, he supervised the preparation of the Air Force program objective memorandum, or POM, which constituted the service's forward financial plan. Second, he sized and managed manpower, acting as the advocate inside the Pentagon and across the Potomac for all the Air Force's personnel requirements. Finally, he oversaw foreign sale of Air Force equipment and support, including training.

Every dollar the Air Force spends and every person working in an Air Force job was part of some "program." Acquisition of a new airplane was a program. Depot maintenance was a program. Buying spare parts was a program. Thus, the Air Force budget included a large number of programs, all of them underfunded, if you listened to the program advocate. The various constituencies in the Air Force—the major commands, support functions, and so forth—had programs they'd struggled to get established and would fight hard to keep, so everybody had a healthy stake in the outcome of each year's program objective memorandum (POM) deliberations. We had an elaborate committee structure in place and an endless spiral of meetings to hear bad news, reprioritize programs, make trades—shuffle, cut and deal again. The structure sought to hammer out compromise and bring a recommended POM to the chief and secretary for annual approval. It was a corporate effort, with the deputy chief for programs and resources refereeing the process.

Forward financial planning can be quite complicated, nearly all programs including a complex set of cost elements. For example, we developed, acquired, bedded down and initially supported a new aircraft using money from several different congressional appropriation categories—research and development, procurement, military construction, and operations and maintenance. Congress branded the money in these funding categories like cattle, and the herds weren't allowed to mix. Managing and keeping track of the funding and manpower elements of all the programs was quite a trick, not made easier by lack of modern management tools. The POM should have been a perfect problem for computers, but we had steam-driven software—fundamentally a fat-finger, spreadsheet approach. There may have been an upside to this since, if we couldn't see into our financial planning very well, neither could anybody trying to supervise us. But I would have risked greater visibility to get a better handle on cost and the question of how to make good trades.

On annual cycles, the near year in the program became the basis for the budget sent to Congress. Budget submission and execution was the business of the Air Force comptroller, located, since the Goldwater-Nichols reforms, not in the Air Staff working for the chief, but in the Secretariat, working for the secretary.

Interestingly, the Air Staff and Secretariat used different accounting software, so it was never certain that what the Air Staff worked so hard to program actually got into the budget in the way we wanted. I had a small group of officers working full time to keep the Secretariat honest, one aspect of the proliferation of management systems, the lack of interoperability and therefore the breakdown of accounting and accountability that occurred in the Pentagon.

Of course, when at last we did get a budget through the Office of the Secretary of Defense (OSD), and then the White House, and finally over to Congress, they changed all the numbers anyway, and we started over. Therefore, regarding a major program that lasted 40 or 50 years, such as, say, the B-52, we did not have one 50-year program, but 50 one-year programs. This was one reason such programs were virtually unmanageable, and why we should be surprised (and grateful) we do not have more cases like the famous $600 toilet seat. When we ended up, as we often did, with a well-trained force or excellent equipment, it was only because lots of people, many of them dedicated civilians, made a creaky system produce in spite of itself.

Even so, rule one of Pentagon budgeting is: everything always costs more than it should. In budget reviews I always assumed it would add cost if we speeded up a program. On the other hand, slowing a program drove up total cost by exposing it to extra out-year price inflation. And, of course, if you wanted to keep a program on schedule, that, too, would cost more money.

Manpower people working for me had the job of sizing the force. Congress voted every year to authorize end strength for each of the services. They did this based on manning requirements we submitted, and they wanted to see some logic in the requests.

My manpower section was also the repository for in-house management expertise. Under the general heading "Total Quality Management," many new techniques (or old ones dressed up as new) were coming into play. The splendid success of Sony, Toyota, and other Japanese firms produced a bumper crop of experts and best-selling books, all offering pointers we'd be foolish to ignore. In any case, we were under some pressure to adopt the "new" management techniques from our civilian leadership. This was a bit of an anomaly, really, because these particular civilians were political appointees, by nature in-and-outers, and in general much less experienced than senior uniformed leadership when it came to management. This would seem counterintuitive, but few civilians get to run organizations with thousands of people, or control multibillion-dollar budgets, whereas such scope is not unusual for military officers. In addition, the Air Force had always run the business side pretty well—even inventing some of these "new" management processes before they were reexported to us from Japan. So I was a bit of a skeptic. But the basic ideas—team building, performance measurement, statistical quality control—were unexceptional, and it cost us little to pay attention to them.

Finally, I supervised Air Force foreign military sales. It was a big business—in the mid-1980s, double-digit billions per year, much of it from the sale of aircraft. We charged overseas customers a 3 percent administrative fee to buy equipment and training for them. Countries like Israel considered themselves sophisticated buyers and opted to avoid the fee, dealing directly with defense contractors, but many others preferred to have the US Air Force in the middle. They knew we'd stand behind any sale made through us, ensuring the equipment met specs and continued to operate.

I did not often involve myself deeply in foreign military sales, mostly a matter of contract administration, but occasionally a sale involved policy or security-classification issues that required attention. In the 1980s, an opening to China occurred. The White House agreed to allow the Chinese government to make large purchases from the Army (long-range artillery), the Navy (ships), and us. The Air Force sale, by far the biggest in dollar terms, was aimed at providing components for an aircraft of indigenous design, the F-8. The Chinese wanted to equip this aircraft with US engines, avionics, and fly-by-wire flight controls. In 1986, I traveled to China for preliminary negotiations and visited Shenyang, location of the plant that would produce the F-8. It was winter, the coal fires were lit, and a quilt of pollution hung over the city, the Chinese not yet panicky about the environment.

I knew something about how airplane factories should look, going back to my days at Ryan Aeronautical in San Diego. The Chinese setup was different. We drove into what seemed a separate village or commune—mud walls, dirt roads, pigs and chickens running loose. Inside a large, ramshackle building suited to producing the Fokker D-5 or the Jenny, parts and subassemblies were stacked seemingly at random. Nearly all the machinery was ancient, though the general manager took pains to show me a few tools he described as "automatic." Indeed, the facility boasted a couple of numerically controlled drills and lathes, maybe two or three generations behind the state of the art. Then workers towed out the prototype F-8, a camel, true committee work: an intake and nose design borrowed from the F-4, a fuselage following the general lines of the Russian Flogger, a tail looking something like the MiG-21's. This baby was ugly, but it was their baby.

The Chinese were said to be difficult to bargain with. They sure seemed in no hurry to close this particular deal, their sense of history's ebb and flow perhaps heightened as compared with ours. They argued hard over every point. After we'd worked through all the issues and just as agreement seemed near, they reopened agenda item number one.

I followed Kissinger's advice: Decide at the outset what terms we'd agree to. Unveil these terms at the first meeting. That's the deal. Do not deviate from the deal. Do not have a fallback position. The deal will be the same on the first day or the last day. If they like the deal, fine. If not, no hard feelings, we'd find something else to do together.

In the end, that's how the negotiation went. They were quickly OK with major items like price and schedule, but the talks dragged out over social issues: How many Chinese could come to the United States? Where would they live? What base facilities would they have access to? Could they shop at the BX? What relationship would they have with the defense contractor doing system integration? (This turned out to be Grumman.) At length, we found suitable answers to all these questions and put together a first-rate program.

Unhappily, Grumman's subsequent performance was second- or third-rate, and the whole deal eventually fell apart after the Chinese had put in a lot of money. They were bitterly (and rightly) disappointed, but the events of 1989—particularly their handling of the Tiananmen Square protests—swept our budding relationship away, as we embargoed military sales to China. Unfortunate. This program could have helped build much-improved relations with a future superpower.

The Air Force was lucky, during this time, to have a secretary, Pete Aldridge, who was superb in every way, including especially a deep understanding of the space business. Though willing to hear us out on any other subject, he regarded space as his sandbox, a position buttressed by his serving concurrently as chief of the National Reconnaissance Office (NRO), the principal agency supervising overhead (satellite) intelligence collection. Since most NRO programs were in the "black" budget, we talked about them only in whispers. They were certainly not subject to the cleansing push and pull endured by ordinary Air Force programs. Aldridge would not allow us to trade off space programs against other essential needs. In fact, quite the reverse. I learned quickly not to fiddle with the 15 percent or so of the Air Force budget that related to space unless Aldridge said OK, which was seldom. If he thought he needed it, Aldridge just put some more of our money into a specific space program of interest and told us to go find an offset somewhere else in the Air Force.

Tommy White, our fourth chief of staff, may have invented the term "aerospace." I never thought there was any such a thing and seldom used the word, being content to write or say "air and space." Hard as we had tried, we hadn't got the places to fit together. "Aerospace" was yet another merchandising concept, in this case one that captured the frigid embrace of an unconsummated marriage.

I'd heard aerospace advocates assert that the Air Force was responsible for that entire big geometry extending from dirt to the sources of cosmic background radiation. Of course, airplanes go up, and there is no obvious place where "up" stops. But this idea that it's all just one big vertical dimension is like thinking the earth's surface is unified because it looks pretty much horizontal, and we can therefore ignore, in organizing armed forces, the subdivisions of land and water, with unsure edges at the coastline.

The seam between Earth's atmosphere and space may be even more tentative, but we know air and space are two different venues. Each occupies a distinctive legal regime: we don't overfly sovereign airspace, whereas we routinely orbit in space above the territory of any state. In a way, a different physics applies: in the atmosphere, the gas laws and Bernoulli's Principle; in space, the ballistics of Newton and Kepler.

Still, someone must be responsible for military aspects of space. Over the years, everybody bid for the job. Gradually the Air Force became the major player, with nearly all military expenditures for space consolidated in our budget, but in many ways this success boomeranged, the space budget being a black hole quite capable of sucking billions of dollars from other critical programs. We should have been more careful here. Fighting in the thin layer of air that clings to Earth is the core competency of the Air Force and needs to be funded first.

Probably the best approach would be to organize a new service department, a Space Force. A less meritorious approach, available if we need an interim solution, would call for two services—an Air

Force and a Space Force—in the Department of the Air Force, following the model of the Navy and Marines in the Department of the Navy. Like the Marines, however, the Space Force should have its own school system and traditions and wear a distinctive uniform—in other words, do all the things that establish service identity and culture, leading to a core competency in space war fighting.

We have so far avoided combat in space, which is fortunate, since the Air Force knows as much about the matter as the Army does about fighting in the air.

The Air Force was conducting a competition to select a primary trainer to replace the T-37. The "Tweety Bird" had been a good, but not great, training aircraft. One of the bad things: it featured side-by-side seating; OK, I guess, for people who go on to crewed aircraft, but just not good for instilling the psychology of self-sufficiency needed in fighter pilots.

Several aircraft had been proposed to replace the T-37, and I got a chance to fly most of them, as did other senior officers having a voice in the selection. One, an aircraft of Argentine manufacture, impressed me with the violence of its spin mode, sort of scaring me. The bird came right out of the spin, but getting it in was a thrill. I had a company test pilot in the back seat and said to him, "OK, I'm going to do that again." He suggested I use a slightly different entry technique, which I did, but it was still a wild ride. Back on the ground, I told him the company had some work to do. He said they knew it and were fixing the problem. A couple of months later, in Argentina, two of their test pilots were killed when they spun one in.

The best airplane in the competition, to my way of thinking, was a Swiss design, the Pilatus P-9. Even though it was propeller driven, performance was better in every respect than the Tweet. However, choosing it would be controversial because a generation earlier the Air Force had selected the T-37 on the argument that all-jet training was a superior way to produce modern pilots. If we switched now to the Pilatus, we'd be seen as walking away from our earlier position.

The virtues of the all-jet training were not obvious to me. In fact, I thought airmanship was better developed through experience with all kinds of aircraft. In addition, a prop job would be considerably cheaper to operate over the life of the system. To the surprise of many, we ended up buying the P-9.

In June 1986, midway through my tour as DCS/PR, Charlie Gabriel retired, and Larry Welch came back from a short stint at SAC to take over as chief of staff. In one of my first contacts with him as the new chief, Welch returned from a meeting downstairs with word that the Reagan defense buildup was over. The FY 86 POM fiscal guidance given to the Air Force showed a reduction from $120 billion to $110 billion, the first downturn in five years.

No doubt about it, the services benefited from the tidal wave of money brought in by the Reagan buildup. Our equipment was in better shape, the backlog of facility repair had been greatly reduced, our readiness was way up, pay had improved, morale was higher. On the other hand, it was true we'd spent much of the near-year funding in haste. We simply couldn't put programs together fast enough to absorb the money in a responsible way. My predecessors as DCS/PR, including Welch himself, had found ways to cubbyhole the money—a billion dollars hidden here, a couple billion squirreled away there, a nice problem for an Air Staff more accustomed to managing shortages. Now we'd start the process of squeezing this fat out of the Air Force program.

Welch called me on a private line with the bad news.

"Don't worry, Chief," I said, "still lots of slack. We can have a great Air Force for a hundred billion dollars."

He knew this already since he had hidden most of the money himself.

Welch asked me to the front office near the end of my second year. He never gave generals a vote on assignments, he said, but he was going to make an exception, just this once. I could either spend another year as the Air Staff programmer, or go to Austin, Texas, and take command of Twelfth Air Force. As for making a fourth star, he thought the choice would not affect my odds, which he did not characterize as either good or bad.

I said, "Let me make sure I understand. I can either stay here in the Pentagon another year or go to Texas and take over Twelfth Air Force?"

Mike Dugan replaced me as DCS/Programs and Resources, at the same time getting his third star.

Chapter 12

Twelfth Air Force

A phenomenon noticeable throughout history regardless of place or period is the pursuit by governments of policies contrary to their own interests . . .

Wooden-headedness, the source of self-deception, is a factor that plays a remarkably large role in government.
—Barbara Tuchman, *The March of Folly*

In the summer of 1987, Twelfth Air Force owned Tactical Air Command's fighter wings west of the Mississippi. One of the largest numbered air forces, Twelfth had about 40,000 people stationed at eight major installations. Its headquarters was at Bergstrom AFB, on the outskirts of Austin, Texas.

Activated in the United States in August 1942, Twelfth Air Force transferred to England in September, where Jimmy Doolittle, recently returned from the Tokyo raid, took command. Subsequently, it supported the Operation Torch landings and fought across North Africa into Sicily and Italy. For a number of reasons, the initial air effort was less effective than it should have been. Our aircrews were up against skilled and experienced Luftwaffe opposition, and, for a while, air base infrastructure favored the other side. Airmen claimed many of the performance shortcomings sprang from command arrangements that prevented concentrating aircraft where they were needed most, that we "parceled out" aircraft to individual ground commanders. Everybody had some airpower, and nobody had enough. We employed flights and squadrons in "penny packets," the phrase made famous by an Army officer, Field Marshal Montgomery. In any case, the first large encounter of US and German combat troops, at the Kasserine Pass during the Tunisia campaign, was such an embarrassment we subsequently centralized control of Allied air units—the RAF's and ours— under Northwest African Air Forces, commanded by Lt. Gen. Carl "Tooey" Spaatz. Thus, Twelfth Air Force had played a starring role in the illumination of a universal truth, the need for central control of airpower in a theater of operations.[18]

Before leaving Washington, I spent a few days TDY at MacDill AFB for a quick checkout in the F-16, our entry, along with the F-15, in the race to build fourth-generation fighters. Known as the Electric Jet, or Viper, the F-16 embodied the triumph of the computer in expanding aircraft-design options and the maturation of the low-bypass turbofan engine.

In the mid-1970s, the Air Force staged a competition for a new "lightweight" fighter. The idea was to balance the high-cost F-15 with something smaller and more affordable so we could outfit more squadrons. The expected outcome would be a large-enough force, with a "high-low mix" of capabilities. In the subsequent flyoff, General Dynamics (later, Lockheed) entered the F-16 against Northrop's F-17. The F-16 turned out to be superior in every respect.

---

18 General Eisenhower, new to senior command during the North Africa campaign, learned some hard lessons. After the war, he was perhaps the most influential supporter of an independent Air Force. And, of course, Tooey Spaatz became our first chief of staff.

It had greater acceleration, could pull more *g*'s, had better range and was less expensive to buy and operate. The airplane went from strength to strength, a very pleasant surprise. We had sought only a highly maneuverable dogfighter, but the F-16 became the most successful dual-role (air-to-air as well as air-to-ground) fighter in history. We ended up with a "high-high" mix.[19]

With the F-16, newish, digital technologies made possible a large number of innovations. The jet featured "relaxed" stability, meaning it would be uncontrollable without onboard computers that constantly monitored flight conditions and made automatic adjustments to keep it stable by artificial means. Relaxed stability gave rise to extraordinary agility. The airframe was stressed for 9 *g*'s and, amazingly, could sustain this load at some weights and configurations without giving away altitude. The ejection seat reclined 30 degrees, giving the pilot a higher heel line, helping prevent blackout by keeping blood from pooling in the boots. It was the first operational aircraft with "fly-by-wire" flight controls, electricity and wiring replacing much hydraulics and plumbing. In place of the familiar control column between the knees, the pilot steered with a side stick that protruded from the right-hand console. Although this side-stick controller had a tiny bit of play, the device seemed rigid, generating inputs for pitch and roll in response to the amount of force applied. It had a head-up display (HUD), a device that put essential information in the front windscreen, level with the pilot's eyes. The combination of a HUD and switches on the stick and throttle that managed the most important weapon control functions meant the pilot never had to look inside, could keep his eyes on the target—could stay "padlocked,"

---

19 The loser in the competition, Northrop's YF-17, evolved into the F/A-18, also a multirole aircraft serving with the Navy, Marines, and several foreign air forces. The F/A-18 never met expectations, eventually being thoroughly redesigned (at great expense) as the F/A-18E/F, after which it continued to be a disappointing performer, in many ways.

as we said. Visibility from the cockpit was exceptional, like sitting outside the airplane. Though not designed for stealth, the jet had built-in signature reduction because of its size and shape. By the turn of the century, F-16s worldwide would compile a combat record of 60 kills and no losses.

I fell in love with the F-16, my all-time favorite airplane. Single engine, single seat, strap it on and go pick a fight. The only bad thing about the jet was its potential for information overload. Even this was a problem only for old guys, like me, throwbacks to the analog, round-dial generation.

By now, the kids were grown and gone. Nearing the end of my Air Staff assignment, we'd bought a Labrador retriever from a well-known kennel in northern Virginia. Still a months-old puppy, Golda made the long drive with us from Washington to Austin. In east Tennessee, where we stopped for the night, she saw deep water for the first time and headed straight for it, belly flopping and swimming by instinct. I tossed a stick; she fetched it—amazing, unlearned behavior. She shook off water in a two-part movement, front to back, one end braced against the quivering of the other.

As the boss at Bergstrom, I got the nicest quarters on base, a modest ranch-style four-bedroom with a large backyard, grassy and enclosed. Flowerbeds bordered the house, the surfaces pro-tected by a mulch of wood and bark. In this backyard, Golda grew into a dignified, gentle companion, one who loved her Milk-Bones but had enough character to invest, burying them under the wood chips for a day or two. Nothing delighted her so much as "finding" one of these, unless it was jogging with me on our runs through a secluded part of the base.

My new boss was TAC's commander, Gen. Bob Russ, a stalwart, mentally and physically. He looked as if he might have played var-sity center for Washington State, which he had. I'd known and respected him for a long time. Russ called me about five minutes after I arrived at Bergstrom: "Go over to the pro shop and buy the best golf clubs they have. I'll be there in a week, and I don't want you blaming your equipment."

I did exactly as he said, making a big mistake. Golf is addictive, and I got hooked. Of course, fighter pilots are not known for moderation. Still, it's lucky I waited until I was 51 years old to start playing golf. Otherwise, I'd be a retired major.

Twelfth Air Force had F-16 wings at Luke, Nellis, and Hill. The commanders of each of these wings were smart enough to have my name painted on one of their airplanes. Usually, when making visits around the command, I climbed in one of these jets. Now, when flying in the western United States, I saw a haze layer in every direction that for the first time looked permanent. Pictures of Earth taken from space show us how thin our layer of air is and ought to make us uneasy about the enormous chemistry experiment we are conducting. We've evolved as a species suited to live only in this air.

Twelfth was the Air Force component of US Southern Command, headquartered in Panama. I therefore had a second job title as commander of US Southern Command Air Forces (COMAFSOUTH), responsible for air operations in Central and South America. In these duties, I reported to an Army four-star, Fred Woerner, an unusually able man, a great example of the Army's foreign area specialist program. In addition to hitting the high spots in a standard infantry officer career track, he was fluent in Spanish, had taken an advanced degree in Latin American studies, had taught the subject, and had spent years in Central and South America in a variety of operational and administrative roles, acquiring experience and expertise that prepared him as well as anything could to head US Southern Command. No one, civilian or military, understood the region and its security issues better than Woerner.[20]

By contrast, I was not so well prepared since, like many Americans, my outward focus was Eurocentric. Now, as when given a piece of the Arab-Israeli problem to work, I hit the books, thought about it, spent time down there, especially in Central America, where one of the last dramas of the Cold War was playing out.

The period 1987–88, my brief tenure as COMAFSOUTH, was a time of tension in Latin America, the countries made increasingly restive by political and social problems of long standing. The region was notorious for the vast economic distance between rich and poor. At college, one of my fraternity brothers was scion of a family that controlled the cement industry and other interests in his Central American country. This young man amused us with tales of how he'd carried a sidearm in public and how he'd had his way with peasant girls. There may have been an element of bravado in this, but we took what he said at face value, knowing the conditions of society there. In the 30 years since my college days—a generation, come to think of it—we had many opportunities to ask ourselves what US interest was served by supporting a status quo so obviously unjust.

Part of the answer, of course, was that in this region we saw ourselves as top dog. Like any status-quo power, we considered change unfavorable and therefore took sides with a tiny, repressive upper class against any reform. Moreover, the rich families, the

---

20 Secretary of Defense Cheney dismissed Woerner in 1989, before Just Cause, the operation that got rid of the Panamanian dictator, Manuel Noriega. Noriega regarded Woerner as an enemy, and a new Bush Administration may have removed him as part of an attempt to mollify Noriega and avoid an invasion. There could have been other reasons, including Woerner's criticism of Washington's performance during the transition from Reagan to Bush, which he described as a policy vacuum making it impossible for us to deal constructively with the political crisis in Panama. In the end, of course, we invaded Panama anyway.

oligarchs, were also citizens, native, and therefore not to be excised by an uprising against foreigners, as colonial rulers in Asia and Africa had been. Because the situation was so much closer to class warfare than imperialism, progressive movements perforce took on the coloration of Marxism—the sense in which reformers were, no doubt, "Communist," or "Communist inspired." However, our preoccupation with the Cold War caused us to be careless: without making a cool assessment of our own long-term interests, we automatically classified every progressive movement as Communist and helped anyone posing as an opponent.

Thus, with our support, the oligarchs remained in control almost everywhere. The exception was Cuba. In 1959, Fidel Castro came to power, replacing an authoritarian government that seemed to have no redeeming qualities. Our hostility helped propel Castro into Khrushchev's embrace. When Castro-inspired guerrilla movements spread through the hemisphere, we saw them primarily in a Cold War context and tried to block any movement to the political left. We invaded the Dominican Republic in 1965, explaining we had to prevent a Cuba-style takeover. In 1970, Salvador Allende was elected president of Chile on a platform of reducing the concentration of wealth. Predictably, we worked hard to destabilize his government and eventually did so. General Pinochet took over and established a military dictatorship that lasted 17 years. The Nixon White House celebrated the coup, but it's hard to see how it furthered our national purposes. Anyway, we ended up backing an unsavory, murderous regime, in most ways the worst enemy of its own people.

We could see the consequences of our uncritical support of brutal and corrupt regimes everywhere, Guatemala perhaps the saddest case. In 1954 Secretary of State John Foster Dulles and his brother, CIA Chief Allen Dulles, overthrew the democratically elected president, Jacobo Arbenz Guzmán, at the behest of the United Fruit Company, a longtime client of Foster Dulles's former New York law firm. Our support of successor military regimes over the next three decades paid off in a staggering death toll as Mayan villages were destroyed wholesale, much of the carnage done under the avuncular eye of Ronald Reagan. Nobody knows how many were killed—maybe 100,000, probably more.

As I took on some responsibility for military operations in the region, the situation in the knot of small, poor Central American countries continued to illustrate our wooden-headedness. In Nicaragua, the Sandinistas had driven out the rapaciously corrupt Somoza regime in 1979. Instead of rejoicing, the Reagan administration cut off aid to Managua and sent support to the Contras, a CIA-guided counterrevolutionary force made up largely of misfit veterans of Somoza's National Guard. The Contras beat up their own people so badly Congress finally got fed up and cut off assistance, but the CIA and others—notably a Marine lieutenant colonel by the name of Ollie North (code name: "The Hammer")—would not let the matter go, continuing to put in money extra legally. (In 1982, following a visit to Nicaragua, Günter Grass famously asked, "How impoverished must a country be before it is not a threat to the US government?") In 1985, the International Court of Justice in The Hague ruled the United States guilty of terrorism (!) against the people of Nicaragua.[21]

Next door, in El Salvador, a civil war had sputtered since 1980, the insurgent force led by the Farabundo Martí National Liberation Front (FMLN). Once again, we sided with far-right political elements responsible for death squads, politically motivated assassinations, and widespread human rights abuse. The FMLN turned for support where it had to, to the Sandinistas, Castro's Cuba, and the Soviet Union itself.

---

21 The Iran-Contra connection is well documented, but there is also much evidence that, despite the Reagan Administration's stentorian pronouncements in connection with the War on Drugs, funding for the Contras was raised by shipping large quantities of cocaine into the United States.

The most important military effort we had under way in Central America was in Honduras, where Southern Command had set up Joint Task Force Bravo at Soto Cano Air Base, a logistics hub sustaining the Contras in Nicaragua and the Salvadoran military in its fight with the FMLN. Soto Cano had lengthy, modern airfield pavements and an Air Force squadron in place doing air traffic control, weather forecasting, fire protection, and civil-engineer support. The full-time Air Force presence belonged to Twelfth Air Force. We also rotated teams through Soto Cano on temporary duty, doing nation building in the surrounding countryside. During my visits there, I spent time both at the base and in the field, watching as we brought medical assistance to remote villages, built landing strips, drilled wells. We were doing some good things but could not expect to offset the damage our national policies caused.

In the Canal Zone, Howard Air Force Base was part of my command. Here, our people were being kicked around—actually physically abused—by Manuel Noriega's police and security services. Noriega rose to the top in Panama through a combination of corruption, blackmail, intimidation, fraud, drug dealing, and murder. Typically, we helped him on the way up because of his cooperation in covert operations against leftists in Nicaragua and El Salvador. Eventually, we could not entirely ignore his criminality—a Florida grand jury returned an indictment on various drug counts—and a falling-out occurred. Noriega reacted by turning his intimidation apparatus, a heavily armed Panama Defense Force and his paramilitary "dignity battalions," on us. Here was a thug we'd bought and paid for over the years, now biting the hand that had fed him. I was responsible for the safety of airmen and their families at Howard, so his bullying got under my skin quickly, not least because I felt so powerless to do anything about it.

Region-wide, overarching, and to some extent subverting our other objectives, the so-called War on Drugs was being prosecuted. (Here, I make intentional use of the passive voice.) It was a "so-called" war because we were trying to persuade impoverished farmers to abandon their only practical cash crop while making no serious effort to reduce our demand for their product. If passage of the Controlled Substances Act in 1970 is a good starting date for the modern War on Drugs, we'd been at it by this time for nearly 20 years. It was impossible to say how much it had cost in dollars, but it had not been cheap, and if the purpose was to decrease drug use in the United States, the "war" seemed to have had the reverse of its intended effect. The whole effort would have been laughable, except so often its impact was to reinforce our alignment with the most repressive and against the most progressive elements in targeted producer societies.

Back at Bergstrom, my headquarters staff was fully manned with representation from all the functional specialties. I had way too many people, about 200, and they were the standard midlevel headquarters mix of a few very good, several pretty good, and lots of indifferent, topped-out résumé writers. The doughnut-shaped headquarters building stood on stilts, an alien design that allowed for parking underneath but otherwise did nothing for productivity.[22] I thought hard about how to energize the place and decided we should do a little war planning. A couple of years before, the Soviets had tried to run crated MiG-21s into Nicaragua in a Bulgarian freighter, the *Bakuriani*. They'd backed off then, but what would we do if Southern Command ever tasked us to run air attacks into Central America? This turned out to be fairly easy to do from western bases, using the F-16 and air refueling. It was also good exercise for a sleepy staff, settled into peacetime routine.

---

22 Sometimes I wondered how we could do something like this, what you might call a hundred-year mistake. But when the base was turned over to the City of Austin to become its international airport and almost all the Air Force structures were torn down, an exception was made for this hovering bagel, kept and converted to a motel.

Just then, former secretary of the Air Force Hans Mark served as chancellor at the University of Texas. He invited Ellie and me to dinner, offering a rather good burgundy produced from grapes grown at the university's own vineyards.

Ninth Air Force was my counterpart organization, commanding TAC's fighter wings east of the Mississippi. By the time I arrived at Twelfth, my friend Chuck Horner had been in command at Ninth for some time. He and my predecessor at Twelfth had established a competition between the two commands, called Long Rifle. Each commander chose a team from one of his wings and staged gunnery events to see who could score better. Horner had won every contest to date. However, I managed to win the only Long Rifle contest staged during my time at Twelfth Air Force.

There were lots of reasons to like Austin. At the navigable limits of the Colorado River, Texas version, it was the eastern gateway to the Hill Country, and a university town, with all that implied for cultural life. Of course, the city was also a center for western music, which had come a long way since Roy Rogers and the Sons of the Pioneers. Countless bars and clubs along Sixth Street featured live acts of all sorts, including, most famously, the "outlaw country" of local hero Willie Nelson. During our time there, Stevie Ray Vaughan, fresh out of rehab, was pounding out a distinctive blues with his band, Double Trouble.

The main thoroughfare, Congress Avenue, was carried across Town Lake by a bridge refurbished in 1980. For years, Mexican free-tailed bats had summered in Austin, roosting at the UT campus, in the capitol building, and elsewhere around town, but the renovated Congress Avenue Bridge had expansion spaces of a size bats could not resist, so now this structure held the largest urban colony in North America. Pregnant females flew in from Mexico in the spring, leaving the males south of the border, and gave birth to pups that learned to fly in about five weeks. By August, clouds

of bats, perhaps a million and a half of them, came pouring out of
the bridge at sunset, an extraordinary sight best watched from one
of the bars along the lake. It could take 45 minutes to empty the
bridge.

The bats were surprisingly popular, not only because they ate
tons of insects every night over a range of 1,000 square miles
around the city, but also because they were a potent tourist attrac-
tion in a town just now rocked back on its heels. Vacant office space
abounded, it was a great time to buy a house—and it wouldn't last.
Texans are different, and one of the ways is that they won't stay
defeated.

I flew the F-16 around to the bases that made up Twelfth Air Force.
I knew all these installations, having been in and out of them often
over the years, but I had to see at first hand what was going on, look
at facilities, assess the senior people. I was deeply involved in managing careers, getting people promoted, working succession plans.

On my first visit to the 366th Wing, at Mountain Home, Idaho,
the commander showed me a construction project nearing completion, a large building going up on the site of a former BX gas station. The commander explained that in its early stages the project
had been delayed by worry about seepage from old underground
fuel tanks. He was proud of having brushed aside these concerns,
ordering the ground above the leaky tanks paved over as part of a
parking lot. I suppose he aimed to show me he was a "can-do" guy.
He was taken aback when I turned out to be one of those tree hug-
gers interested in protecting the environment.

To be fair, this wing commander was a good officer (and a future
general officer) whose attitude was representative. Nonetheless, I
knew then and know now no good reason the Air Force's mission
requires us to be thoughtless about the natural environment.

Larry Welch asked that I represent him at *El Grito*, Mexico's
Independence Day celebration. Dignitaries from throughout the

hemisphere gathered in Mexico City for a parade and round of parties. Manuel Noriega was there, Miss Panama of 1988 on his arm. Two or three tough-looking security people shadowed him. At the time, he was being very ugly with our people in Panama, so I fantasized about having a go at him, and actually got my chance late one evening. At a reception held in the city hall, Ellie and I strolled out on a third-floor balcony, and there was Noriega, sans bodyguards. Just the three of us in the moonlight, and I could have thrown the son of a bitch over the railing.

But I chickened out.[23]

On 20 February 1988, we lost an F-16 at Luke. Coming off a practice bombing run at high speed, the aircraft was bounced by Navy fighters acting as surrogate adversaries. With lots of energy and a light load, the pilot made a max-*g* turn into the attack. A review of his HUD film seemed to indicate an immediate loss of consciousness, the *g* relaxing as the aircraft descended to impact. In the subsequent mishap investigation, we learned the pilot was a distance runner, a marathoner, logging perhaps 50 road miles a week. If anything, he'd been too dedicated to this activity. His boss had suggested he cut back a bit—advice he probably did not follow. He was tall and slender anyway, and the running gave him very high aerobic fitness, just the sort of physical profile increasing the risk of *g*-induced loss of consciousness, or *g*LOC (pronounced "G-lock").

Under a *g* load, centrifugal forces flush blood from the brain and chest, sending it south to the feet. The F-16's leaned-back seat was designed to impede this flow, and the pilot could help by straining and tightening stomach and thigh muscles to squeeze or constrict

---

23 When Guillermo Endara won an election in 1989, Noriega annulled it, citing a massive US effort to influence the outcome. We subsequently invaded Panama and removed Noriega to the United States, where he was tried and convicted of drug trafficking and sentenced to 40 years in federal prison.

veins and arteries. Even so, most humans can't take 9 g's. The brain shuts down quickly if it does not receive a more-or-less continuous supply of oxygen, which it won't if blood stops being delivered. The critical measurement is the height of the pipe running from the heart to the brain. The longer this distance, the harder it is for the heart to pump oxygen uphill. Tall people therefore have a built-in disadvantage in any g-pulling contest.

Long ago, we learned that aerobic fitness expands the throughput capacity of the blood-delivery system—good for normal, 1-g health. However, fighter pilots don't need their blood to slosh around quite so freely, so we had encouraged anaerobic fitness, going so far as to install weight-lifting gear in fighter squadrons. In combination with weight work, a moderate amount of running is OK. Our Luke pilot's training regime had not been in the moderate category.

Not much in the way of realistic ground training can improve human performance under a g load. We can lecture about the problem, but only one training device—the centrifuge—subjects a pilot to the loads encountered in high-g flight. The Air Force had a couple of centrifuges, and riding in them had become more common as we tried to figure out how to deal with modern, 9-g airplanes. Such training was not yet universal in the fighter community, a situation I resolved to correct, at least in Twelfth Air Force. To establish priorities, I asked for a computer run to identify fighter pilots who were tall, slender, and had not ridden in the centrifuge. My own name appeared high on this list.

I reported to the centrifuge, located at Brooks AFB, near San Antonio. After a brief period of platform instruction on the grunting and straining maneuvers that increase g tolerance, I climbed in the capsule and got spun around in a g profile that went up and down, climaxing in a sustained load of 9 g's. It was tough going, recorded by technicians so we could take the videotape home and watch ourselves fall asleep.

Like giraffes, pilots fight with their heads, the one with the longest neck needing to do so carefully. The big message: As a combat system, we are a blend of limitations, ours and the machine's. The lower limit always prevails.

Riding the centrifuge was not much fun—more in the category of hard work. (I decided everybody in Twelfth Air Force got to go once before I went twice.) In addition, most people end up with what we called "*g* measles," a sort of rash that shows up on the backside and underarms when the weight of blood bursts tiny capillaries in the skin. However, pilots can in fact increase their *g* tolerance by training, and the centrifuge was the best equipment we had for doing this.

On 3 June 1988 I presided at the commissioning of Air Force ROTC cadets at San Diego State, now a university. Though they'd certainly forgotten, it was a sort of forgiveness to invite me back since, as a cadet, I'd narrowly avoided being thrown out of the program on account of my distaste for the parade ground.

Also in June, I returned to Grants Pass, Oregon, for my high school's hundred-year anniversary celebration. I was among 100 (mostly living) former "Cavemen" named to the Centennial Hall of Fame. The invitation proclaimed a black tie event. I should have been suspicious. It was no longer true that the timber industry provided most local employment, but the town still showed its lumberjack roots and, in any case, the event venue was the school gymnasium. Having taken the invitation at face value, I turned up in Mess Dress uniform, medals and all, and felt pretty foolish.

I was at Bergstrom 13 months, leaving on promotion to become commander in chief of Pacific Air Forces.

Logbook: Bergstrom, 1987–88

F-16A	157.1
F-16B	22.9
Total F-16	180.0

Chapter 13

Pacific Air Forces

What we may be witnessing is not just the end of the Cold War, or the passing of a particular period of postwar history, but the end of history as such: that is, the end point of mankind's ideological evolution and the universalization of Western liberal democracy as the final form of human government.

—Francis Fukuyama, "The End of History"

Pacific Command stretched from the west coast of America to the east coast of Africa, a huge part of the globe—more than 100 million square miles—spanning 16 time zones and containing 40 countries and 60 percent of the world's population. As a joint command, PACOM had the normal service components: Army, Navy, Air Force, and Marines. In addition, it had a special operations component (joint special operations task force, or JSOTF) and subunified joint commands responsible for US forces in Japan (USFJ) and Korea (USFK). As commander in chief of Pacific Air Forces (CINCPACAF), I ran the Air Force component, with administrative responsibility for our units stationed in Japan, Korea, the

Philippines, Guam, and Hawaii. The major organizations under my command included three numbered air forces—Fifth (Japan), Seventh (Korea), and Thirteenth (Philippines)—and, locally, the 15th Air Base Wing, which operated Hickam Field, site of my headquarters, collocated with the international airport at the west edge of Honolulu.

Like all component commanders, I reported up two chains of command. For military operations in-theater, my boss was the commander in chief of Pacific Command (CINCPAC), by tradition a Navy admiral. Initially, Ron Hays filled this post. Soon after I arrived, Hunt Hardisty replaced Hays. Both men were naval aviators and good guys with whom I enjoyed excellent working relations.[24] I was on a first-name basis with both, which hadn't happened before in my career. (Across service lines, there seemed to be no rank among four-stars.) For administration—the Title 10 functions of "organize, train, and equip"—I answered to Secretary of the Air Force Don Rice and Chief of Staff Larry Welch. (Inside the Air Force, we had a dozen four-stars, and none of us called the chief of staff anything but "Chief.")

Notwithstanding my friendship with the boss, there was an element of intellectual dishonesty in calling PACOM a joint command. In Hawaii, conveying real estate by leasehold rather than fee simple was still a common practice. Buyers purchased a right to occupy the buildings for a while but never got ownership of the ground, a system designed to protect the power of the original missionary families who had acquired vast tracts of land. Concerning the Pacific area of responsibility (AOR), the Navy's approach

---

24 I got along well with Hardisty, in particular. He was a naval aviator of some note. In 1961, a young Lt. Hunt Hardisty flew an F-4 to a world speed record of 784 knots (Mach 1.2) over a hazardous 3 km low-level course (maximum altitude 100 meters). This exceeded the previous such record, set eight years earlier, by more than 130 knots. It was a gutsy performance, there still being some unanswered stability and control issues with the airplane.

With Ellie, Brian, and Mark, Langley Field, Christmas, 1983.

1983, Bill Creech and Ellie pin on a second star.

*1985,
Charlie Gabriel
and Ellie pin on
a third star.*

*Kuala Lumpur, 1986. "You Are My Sunshine,"
Larry Welch and two future Air Force chiefs sing for their
supper on a trip through the Far East. Standing next
to me, Mike Ryan, then Welch's executive officer.*

*Twelfth Air Force commander, Bergstrom Field, 1988,
with the "Long Rifle" I won from Chuck Horner.*

*Flying my
all-time favorite
airplane, the F-16.*

matched that of the missionaries. The theater was mostly salt water the Navy thought it had bought and paid for during World War II. It tolerated the presence of the other services only so long as we played Tonto to their Lone Ranger. Thus, an admiral had headed PACOM through all the years of its existence, a situation creating dissonance between claimed jointness and lived reality. One way to make the command truly joint would be to rotate the top job among the services, an idea guaranteed to gag the Navy. Presumably, there had never been a soldier, airman, or Marine who could handle the work.[25]

Hawaii was a grand assignment. My duties proved enjoyable and not especially stressful. In their respective AORs, responsibility for air operations had been decentralized to the numbered air forces. These three commands were smaller in every way than my old outfit, Twelfth Air Force, but their senior officers all had joint or Alliance duties that added to their standing and workload. In Japan, Lt. Gen. J. B. Davis led Fifth Air Force as well as US Forces Japan, the subunified command of PACOM. His headquarters was at Yokota Air Base, on the Kanto Plain, some 30 miles northwest of Tokyo. Davis's principal operating units included the 18th Wing at Kadena, Okinawa, and the 432nd Wing at Misawa, in northern Honshu.

As commander of USFJ, Davis was also responsible for a variety of diplomatic and political contacts with the US Embassy and Japanese government. J. B. was an unusually able officer, as popular

---

25 Over the years, when asked to nominate officers to command the "joint" Pacific Command, the Air Force understood that no one other than a Navy candidate would be accepted. But during the Vietnam War, we sent Jack Ryan to run PACAF. Ryan had already headed Strategic Air Command for two years and was a future Air Force chief of staff. Toward the end of his PACAF tour, we nominated Ryan (unsuccessfully) for overall command in the Pacific. Since he was so obviously a superior candidate, the Navy about had a fit.

as any commander I'd known and very effective with the ambassador and country team, and with the Japanese. He was agile, quick to patch up injury to the international relationship inflicted by airmen, sailors, and Marines at our outsized operations in the main islands and, especially, on Okinawa.

Okinawa occupied strategic geography, almost equidistant from Tokyo, Seoul, Hong Kong, Taipei, Shanghai, or Manila. If there was trouble at any of the Pacific's hot spots, our forces on Okinawa were only hours away. So, this small island, accounting for less than 1 percent of Japan's land area, had since World War II hosted two-thirds of the American presence. Many Okinawans were unhappy about it. We were noisy, damaged the environment, had accidents, maybe stored nuclear weapons. Our young servicemen committed offenses the Okinawan police and courts were powerless to remedy under terms of the extraterritoriality arrangements worked out with Tokyo, a situation particularly galling for Okinawa, once an independent nation known as the Kingdom of the Ryukyu Islands, with its own language and religious beliefs. (An Imperial ban on weapons led to the development of Okinawa's most famous cultural export, karate.) Tension was not eased by the perception that Tokyo was quite content to concentrate American forces on Okinawa rather than in the main islands. Nobody had ever dealt with the range of exotic issues arising from this relationship better than J. B. Davis.

In Korea, my old buddy from MacDill—Buck Rogers, now a three-star—commanded Seventh Air Force. His headquarters was collocated with the 51st Fighter Wing at Osan, a few miles south of Seoul. His other major tactical unit, the 8th Fighter Wing, was farther down the peninsula at Kunsan. Like J. B. Davis in Japan, Buck wore a couple of hats. On the joint side, he was deputy to the commander of US Forces Korea, an Army four-star. In case of hostilities, his Alliance role was commander, Combined Air Command, responsible for integrating operations of the US and Korean air forces. Buck was turning in a typically solid performance.

Thirteenth Air Force, at Clark Air Base, north of Manila, was commanded by a two-star—Don Snyder, another fine officer and experienced fighter jock. Snyder supervised the 3rd Wing at Clark and PACAF's largest training program, Cope Thunder. Patterned after TAC's Red Flag, Cope Thunder gave pilots an opportunity to participate in complex, large-scale maneuvers, providing a reasonably safe way to do realistic training designed to correct the many performance deficiencies revealed in Vietnam. Because of the long distances involved, PACAF units could not often deploy back to Nellis for Red Flag, so we'd set up this look-alike program at Clark. Fighter units from all over PACAF—indeed, from the Navy and other regional air forces, notably Singapore's—came to Clark to participate in Cope Thunder.

Snyder, too, had responsibilities extending outside the Air Force. In Manila, he worked with the US country team, trying to build ties with a new and distrustful Philippine government. He brought common sense to our not-always-easy relations with the US Navy, which had a major installation at Subic Bay. South and east of the Philippines, Snyder represented us well, conducting exercises and operations as needed in Australia, Indonesia, Malaysia, and Singapore. Prior to my arrival, Thirteenth Air Force played a key role in extracting Ferdinand and Imelda Marcos as their regime toppled, bringing them first by helicopter to Clark and then by long-range transport back to Hickam, where they stayed awhile in VIP quarters, running up a legendary (and never paid) phone bill.

Hawaii's law mandated a four-month quarantine for canine immigrants. I brought Golda over to begin her sentence early, depositing her in the state's isolation facility. Audrey Wages, wife of Col. Brian Wages, a friend working on the PACAF staff, volunteered to visit daily. Nevertheless, Golda must have wondered where she went wrong. After we got to the islands, Ellie and I took up visitation duties, one or both of us sitting in the pen with Golda for a while each day. Ecstatic to see us coming, she was devastated each time we left. At length, the happy day arrived. Time served, she was paroled under our supervision and, true to character, forgave us immediately.

During the obligatory courtesy call on Governor John Waihee, I asked about the pet quarantine. He said the islands had never had a case of rabies. Point made, I suppose, but he'd never met Golda.

★★★★

With USAF operations in-theater decentralized and in competent hands, it was easy to fall into the monitoring mode. I followed an old habit of arriving at work by 7:00 a.m., already 1:00 p.m. Washington time. By noon, here in Hawaii, the Pentagon was closed for normal business. I could go to the gym or go home early for an afternoon walk with Ellie and Golda.[26]

I found another great way to spend afternoons: flying with the Hawaii Air National Guard (HANG). I'd stopped at Luke on my way from Twelfth to PACAF and checked out in the F-15, a wonderful air-to-air fighter, its pure Air Force design a gift after years of being stuck with the F-4. The HANG had an F-15 squadron at Hickam, so I asked if I could maintain currency with them. They smiled in a way that said many other PACAF commanders had hung their helmet and *g*-suit at the squadron, never to be seen again. They were surprised (and, I think, pleased) when I showed up regularly, concentrating on the basic air-to-air scenarios, mostly "1 v. 1." I would have liked to progress to more sophisticated combat profiles, but these required greater situation awareness and overall proficiency than I ever attained. The HANG's best pilots were mighty good, and I spent a lot of time looking over my shoulder at some Guard guy parked at my six o'clock. Over a

---

26 In Khabarovsk, 500 miles north of Vladivostok, my counterpart at Soviet Far East Air Force headquarters was seven time zones ahead of Moscow. Many of the phone calls he presumably got during Moscow's normal duty hours cut into his sleeping time, one of many reasons he must have envied my circumstances.

27-month tour, I averaged three sorties a month with the HANG, a great outfit I was proud to be part of.

Because I flew so much with the Guard, when I went forward to visit regular combat units, I could jump immediately into the F-15C without having to reestablish landing currency in the two-seat F-15D. My flying as a wingman in local exercises at Kadena, in Korea, and at Cope Thunder in the Philippines made, I think, a positive impression with aircrews, and even on the chiefs of regional air forces. For too many air forces, flying was something done by juniors, blue-collar work abandoned as soon as practical. I undercut this view when I taxied up and parked a single-seat jet.

For longer-range transport around the theater, I had two modified KC-135 tanker aircraft that were configured for VIP support. They had office space and a small bedroom in back, with first-class seating for a dozen or so staff. The two aircraft supported both CINCPAC and me, with the boss getting priority in case of conflict (which careful scheduling avoided during my tour). I got a quick, one-ride checkout in the bird, making a dozen or so touch-and-goes. I'd always fly the aircraft with an IP in the right seat, so there was no requirement for more elaborate training. Over the next two years or so, I'd make every takeoff, climb to initial level-off altitude, turn the aircraft over to the IP and go back to the office. My staff brought the paperwork I needed to catch up on, so those long, transpacific legs were ideal for cleaning out the in-basket. A steward came around just before descent, waking me if necessary, so I could go back up and make the letdown, approach, and landing. It was more transportation than flying, and I should have felt bad about doing all the fun stuff. But I didn't.

Back at Hickam, I worked on a new passion: golf. In this theater, golf was not an elective but a professional qualification, without which I'd have had almost nothing in common with many counterpart air chiefs in the AOR. I silently thanked Bob Russ for insisting

I get started on the sport a year earlier. Golf is a hard game, disguised as easy. I had very little talent for it, but with lots of time, an 18-hole course of my own, and ambitious subordinates conceding putts, my handicap shrank a bit.

I was invited to participate in the pro-am for the Hawaii Open. Play backed up, and I observed tee shots of the foursome ahead, which included the football celebrity O. J. Simpson. He seemed a strong player but had a temper that detonated into a cloud of profanity with every errant drive, of which there were plenty. Not a high draft choice for golfing partner.

Like Israel, Honolulu was a village. We ran into the same people at every social event. I learned quickly who I should talk to when the Air Force needed something from the community. Aside from that, society here was exotic and intriguing, with much to show the rest of us, especially about racial diversity. Only one in five residents of Honolulu was white, one in 10, a native Hawaiian. Nearly half the population was Asian, mostly Japanese. The atmosphere was relaxed and laid-back. People got along nicely, the tension drained from relationships. They seemed to have thought about it and at a certain point decided race wasn't all that big a deal, the attitude somehow now taken for granted, part of the scenery.

A nascent Hawaiian sovereignty movement bubbled just below the surface, rooted in anger about the imperial past and touching race only secondarily. As it turned out, not everybody was happy about Queen Liliuokalani being overthrown in 1893, about the annexation of 1898, or about what some viewed as a prolonged military occupation since. The grant of statehood in 1959 did not entirely erase these concerns. Mainland America hadn't paid much attention, but should have. So far, the independence movement had been nonviolent, but these islands have produced some fine warriors.

Napoleon said administration was half of a general's work, the estimate being in the nature of a complaint. Administration gets no respect, skill at it vastly underappreciated. But his observation does underscore the activity's importance, even seems a little light. Supervising the functions, the management "tail" of a military organization, is almost all administration. Who will we recruit, retain, educate, promote, retire? Who will we assign? Where? What bases will we close; what new ones build? What equipment and supplies will we purchase; what old equipment will we sell, store, demolish? Answering these and many other questions is hard work, unglamorous, often unrewarding but, at a certain level, too important to be delegated.

The trick is to figure out what can be delegated. Part of a general's work—a large part—is to make sure sergeants and lieutenant colonels also do their work. This task, too, is largely administration.

A lot of fun and a wonderful assignment, but what should I be working on? Naturally, there were the normal administrative problems of any large headquarters. A considerable volume of budget, legal, and personnel actions came by for review. I gave close attention to assignments, particularly those of senior personnel. When time came to rotate Buck Rogers out of Korea, I pulled in Ron Fogleman, an old friend going back to Misty days, and got him promoted to three-star.

The Pacific contained some of the globe's most beautiful real estate, and we had not been particularly good stewards of it. When I first went to Johnston Island, owned by the Air Force but site of a proposed Army chemical-munitions disposal plant, I drove by a large, open pit hard by the ocean, into which we had for years dumped commercial waste. Andersen AFB, in Guam, presented another troubling case. For decades, we had simply tipped trash of all sorts over a scenic bluff, down its sides and out of view. In haste, I made sure commanders knew I'd get even for any such practice and began to budget and spend the money needed for site remediation all over the theater.

I also had an issue with the quantity and character of classified material held by the headquarters. Any staff officer worth his building pass had a set of rubber stamps up to at least top secret and overclassified everything but the most routine documents. This happened in part because people regard their work as important and in part because it's easier than thinking about proper classification. Periodically all headquarters were supposed to reduce the size of classified holdings. Naturally, we searched out best practice, established metrics and collected data proving we were doing better, all without noticeable impact on the Niagara of classified paperwork.

I knew we lost track of genuinely important documents because trivial ones choked the system, so I decided to reduce classified materials by directing every office to empty and turn in one-third of the safes used for secure storage. The base newspaper ran a picture of me standing in one of Hickam's spacious maintenance hangars next to more than 400 heavy, three-drawer safes that had been liberated.

When everything is secret, nothing is secret.

A manager administers (time cards, head count, budgets), maintains (real property, records, files), and works to bring stability, or at least a semblance of order, to the arrangement of things. By contrast, leadership concerns people. Leaders communicate with people, give responsibility to people, inspire commitment in people. A leader experiments, innovates, takes risks—may in fact reduce stability as he seeks new ways to get the job done.

Does this mean leadership is more important than management? I don't think so. The combination of strong leadership and weak management is no better, and may be worse than the reverse. Anyway, the two skills overlap considerably. The Great Safe Turn-In would seem an example of management, work concerning things— and it was. But it was also a small stimulus to change, a teaching exercise, a signal to people.

Our interaction with other service components was interesting. The Navy component was called Pacific Fleet, and its commander was Adm. David Jeremiah. A University of Oregon ROTC graduate, Dave came in the Navy, got out, returning to civilian life, then reentered. It just doesn't happen that a non-Annapolis, broken-service guy makes it to four stars in the Navy. That Jeremiah had done this was all anyone needed to know about his capacity. He was from the surface ship (as opposed to aviation or submarine) part of the Navy, and I liked him very much, even though his heart pumped seawater.

The Navy was the major leagues in the Pacific, but all the services were here in strength. Having bounced up and down on the matter, the Air Force now saw the importance of senior representation and sent a four-star. The Army had a three-star component commander, also stationed in Hawaii, his lower rank reducing his service's clout in joint, on-island deliberations. The Army did have a four-star in the AOR, but he was in Korea, with a variety of job titles allowing him to finesse CINCPAC when the going got rough. The Army did not relish having its senior officer in-theater answer to an admiral. Neither MacArthur nor Westmoreland ever felt the need to report through Honolulu. Whenever conditions allowed, the Army managed to carve out a separate unified command. No such problem existed for the Marine Corps, which had three-star representation and no ax that needed grinding in Hawaii.

I got along well with the other service component commanders but only so-so with the Joint Special Operations Task Force (JSOTF) commander, who at the time happened to be an Air Force one-star. He led a subunified command that included some Army Snake Eaters, Navy SEALS, and a few Air Force support aircraft stationed in Okinawa. I didn't like the idea that he controlled in-theater Air Force assets independent of me. In addition, JSOTF had outstanding people and capabilities that should have been better integrated with service components in order to use them properly in theater war.

Regarding the Special Operations Force (SOF), the services have only themselves to blame for its creation. For years we systematically neglected the need for highly trained specialists to conduct deep raids, hostage rescues and the like. The Army's attitude was particularly ambivalent. The fact that Delta Force belonged to them was offset by the distaste many senior officers felt for anything that smacked of an "elite." Many in the Army saw their institution as a reflection of America, a cross-section rather than a privileged cream of the crop, an attitude giving the Marine Corps, the "un-Army," a recruiting edge with young men who wanted to be different. But the antipathy was seen also in the other services. As late as 1987, the Air Force had never promoted to general any officer who might be considered a career special operator.

Thus, special operations capabilities languished, creating a vacuum politicians moved into. President Kennedy started it, making a darling of Green Berets he preferred to an incurably orthodox military hierarchy. The role, size, and organization of Special Forces became a political issue, largely impervious to straight thinking.

If we could start with a clean sheet of paper, the services should be merged into a single armed force, with everybody wearing the same uniform. Inside that unified structure, force capabilities ought to be organized against the range of possible military tasks. A special unit would be formed to conduct high profile, risky, but small-scale operations, like antiterrorism or hostage rescue. This unit would incorporate the seagoing and air support elements needed to accomplish its mission. Everyone involved would live, train and practice their trade together. For the moment, this ideal of organizational design is out of reach.

An alternative approach would be to direct the Army to build such an organization, in-house. Delta Force was and is the ground-based foundation of such an enterprise, and air and naval support capabilities could have been grafted to it, with the people wearing Army uniforms and working and playing together, the formula for producing durability and cohesion.

Lacking its own capability, Delta Force was obliged to reach across departmental seams for essential support, a fatal flaw that produced, for instance, the collapse at Desert One of the 1980 "Eagle Claw" operation mounted by the Carter Administration to rescue American hostages held in Iran. The Desert One failure, more than anything else, led to the creation of the joint Special Operations Command (SOCOM.)

By definition, missions like hostage rescue ought to be relatively small, stealthy, and precise. They need to be all these things because success will depend on achieving operational surprise. (Often such operations will break down anyway, owing to inherent risk or difficulty in execution, but failure should not be traceable to faulty organization, as was the case for the doomed Eagle Claw.)

Foreign internal defense is another good role for the Special Operations Force. This is the job of building up the domestic armed forces in a friendly country. It's a "go there and stay there" mission, a full-time assignment where you become part of the landscape, with language skills and cultural understanding of great importance.

In a conventional war, the SOF will be very useful operating behind enemy lines. First, SOF can conduct certain types of surgical operations beyond the capability of air. They can attack concealed targets or safe havens, can damage but not destroy a target, or take out target system operators but leave the equipment intact. Second, SOF can operate in a cooperative role with air. They can infiltrate and designate targets visually, electronically, or optically. They can locate moving or perishable targets, positively identify them and hand them off to air for attack. Finally, SOF can help with certain other kinds of enhancements of the air campaign, like recovery of downed airmen. Obviously, all these activities need to be integrated with the other combat actions occurring at depth in a conventional battlefield. Such integration is absolutely essential to ensure the effectiveness and safety of everybody involved. For me, "integrated with" means "commanded by," command being the surest tool for producing integration. That is, when it operates deep in Type A conventional war, SOF should probably report to the Air Force component commander.

The operational roles envisioned here are relatively small-scale—antiterrorism, hostage rescue, foreign internal defense, participation as an auxiliary in the deep battle—commonly involving teams consisting of a handful of men, certainly no more than a few hundred at most. But with the inclusion of the Army's Rangers, the SOF has become rather large—as this is written, more than 60,000 soldiers, sailors, airmen, and Marines committed—a bigger combat force than can contemporaneously be fielded by, for example, Great Britain.

Moreover, expansion of the SOF has siphoned off military skills required in the routine operations of the regular service components. For example, when the Navy is tasked to conduct boarding and takedown operations as part of a blockade, they need SEAL teams now available only in the Special Operations component. As for the Rangers, what's "special" about them is that they are highly trained and motivated light infantry, experts in direct action, airfield seizure, ambushes, and interdiction raids. These shock troops may be the best night-fighting force in the world. Unlike the Special Forces, who must speak foreign languages and train and advise other countries' military forces, Rangers are strictly fighters. If they are not part of the Army component in a theater of operations, we ought to ask ourselves what it is we want the Army for.

It bears repeating that the organization of the SOF, like that of the Marine Corps, contains much merit when, but only when, it operates alone. The big problem comes when the SOF must act in concert with the regular service components in joint operations, in which case it represents another army and another air force, and even to some degree another navy, that needs integration with conventional forces. To reduce organizational complexity, the sworn enemy of battlefield success, what should happen in conventional, Type A conflict is that much, if not most, of the SOF is broken up and elements of it returned to and put under the command of regular service component commanders.

Well, perhaps the SOF is so well organized as a joint force that we want it to command more-or-less conventional military operations up to a certain size, wherever they occur.[27] This might be part of the answer to the so-far unsolved problem of how to handle Type B War. If so, the SOF has a direct competitor in the Marine Corps, also a joint force in readiness. (This is the reason the Marines were so reluctant for so long to commit any part of the Corps to the SOF.) The Special Operations component of a joint command might take on any operational mission, helped as needed by the regular service components in-theater, or the CONUS-based SOCOM might deploy forces and take charge of conventional operations in a theater, again supported by the regular service components. (Either of these alternatives makes the in-place joint theater commander a sort of fifth wheel, a redundant reporting layer.) For major conflict in a theater of operations the SOF would still be too small, unless we do away with the regular service components and all join the SOF—maybe not such a bad idea.

The operational difficulty of integrating the SOF has been complemented by a congressional grant of budgeting authority to the Special Operations Command. SOCOM now has its own Major Force Program (a special budget tracking category) and direct congressional authorization and appropriation lines. Therefore SOCOM (and its service components) needs the full panoply of staff support to manage requirements and monitor programming, budgeting, and equipment acquisition, just as if it were an entirely separate service. As a result, SOCOM headquarters end strength now certainly exceeds the manpower requirements of any reasonably sized raid or hostage-rescue operation.

---

27 This seems to be the way we are moving, the secretary of defense having proclaimed that the SOF can be the supported command in a theater of operations.

Today, the Special Operations Force is proud to claim that it is trained and equipped to respond across the spectrum of security threats around the globe. And that, of course, is exactly the problem. It needs to be reshaped so that it responds to "special" threats—counterterrorism, hostage rescue, and foreign internal defense being the premier roles here envisaged—that are beyond the scope of the regular armed forces. For the United States, the SOF now constitutes a third, competing, and better-organized army. Like the (also better-organized) Marine Corps, it would be improved by becoming smaller. If, like Kennedy, we're unhappy with the Army, we should fix the Army, not keep it and hire substitutes to do its work.

Incidentally, counterinsurgency and nation building are a big jump from foreign internal defense and well beyond what we should expect of the SOF. The skills required—police, civil affairs, government, psychological operations, engineers, intelligence, signals, medical—must come from regular active and reserve forces. Especially useful, in my view, are engineers who do road construction, well drilling and similar tasks, and medical teams who deliver care in remote locations. This sort of activity can and should be done on a short term (TDY), project-oriented basis, not by special operators who go and stay, becoming part of the culture. The SOF might operate in support, but we should exclude counterinsurgency and nation building from its primary roles.

Returning to the question of what I should be doing, there were a couple of world-class problems that needed fixing. One, already mentioned, was that CINCPACAF—and, for that matter, Europe's CINCUSAFE, the other major overseas air commander—did not own all of the airpower in the AOR. Naturally, I couldn't expect to command air elements of the other services, which properly should have been unified to a much greater degree within the newly established Air Force in 1947. That was bad enough. But I didn't even command all the air units my own service kept in-theater, the Air Force special operations aircraft assigned to JSOTF being but one example. On Okinawa, the base at Kadena showcased the issue. Here, PACAF's 18th Fighter Wing served as the host unit, but several large tenants (as well as numerous smaller detachments) reported up various stovepipes running to headquarters outside PACAF: An Airborne Warning and Control System (AWACS) squadron belonged to Tactical Air Command; a tanker wing, to Strategic Air Command; a rescue unit was part of Military Airlift Command. On Guam, smack-dab in the middle of the Pacific AOR, Andersen AFB belonged to SAC, a legacy of the Vietnam years when Arc Light attacks staged from there. The principal unit stationed with Fifth Air Force at Yokota—a C-130 wing—reported to MAC. In all, about 80,000 Air Force people lived and worked in the Pacific, but only 60,000 of them reported to me. Thus, we had not managed even to integrate the Air Force in this theater of operations, making nonsense of our primary doctrinal claim that control of airpower should be centralized.

On Okinawa and elsewhere, cleaning up the jurisdictional mess would require reorganization of the entire Air Force, something obviously exceeding my authority, but when I raised the issue of Guam's Andersen AFB with SAC's boss, Jack Chain, he willingly handed it back to Pacific Command, a surprising and appreciated act of statesmanship.

The second major problem was Alaska. The Air Force had felt for a long time that Alaska should be part of Pacific Command. Some years before my arrival in Honolulu, the same Jack Chain, then on the Air Staff as deputy chief for plans and operations, had traveled north with the task of convincing Alaskans (notably Senator Ted Stevens) that they should volunteer to become part of PACOM. Chain was unceremoniously shown the door. Still bitter about the loss of Kiska and Attu early in World War II, Alaskans believed that the "pineapple admirals" down in Honolulu had given up these islands. Nevertheless, the geography was straightforward. Alaska fit into the Pacific, and carving it out as separate from PACOM didn't make military sense.

Lt. Gen. Tom McInerney, an extraordinarily able officer, was serving in Alaska as commander of Alaskan Air Command. I'd known and admired Tom since he was a lieutenant. A standout fighter pilot in our initial cadre of Phantom drivers, Tom did much to introduce the F-4 successfully into the Air Force. Early in his career, he published some fine articles on weapons and tactics. He had an outstanding combat record and a brilliant Pentagon tour working fighter requirements. With first-rate social skills, Tom got more done in five minutes at a cocktail party than most of us accomplished in a 40-hour workweek, making some (me included) envious and others both envious and resentful. He was almost too good.

If Alaska were to become part of Pacific Command, Tom would experience a considerable downgrade. Instead of reporting to the chief of staff as head of a major air command, he would report to me. Nevertheless, Tom understood it was better for both the Air Force and the country to bring Alaska into PACOM. He and I talked the matter over, agreed, and conspired to get it done.

I made several trips to Alaska, meeting opinion makers in Anchorage and Fairbanks. In Washington, I conferred with Senator Stevens and Hawaii's Senator Dan Inouye, seniors in their respective parties who rotated chairmanship of the Defense Subcommittee of the Appropriations Committee. Of course, Inouye had nothing to lose by Alaska's coming under a command headquartered in Honolulu. It was Stevens I had to convince.

I brought a planeload of Alaskan community leaders to Hawaii to meet with my local Civilian Advisory Committee. We put together a full program, business and social (golf!). I also flew Honolulu leaders up to Anchorage, during summertime, of course. The groups liked each other, and I got their endorsement. Senator Stevens came around; he admired and trusted Tom McInerney, and that tipped the scales. The Air Force disestablished Alaskan

A brand new CINCPACAF, interviewed by Armed Forces TV, Korea, 1988.

Flying the F-15, with the Hawaii Air National Guard.

*1989, Chief of Staff
Larry Welch
makes a point.*

*1989, with Tom McInerney (commander, Alaskan Air Command),
Bob Russ (commander, Tactical Air Command),
and Mike Dugan (commander, US Air Forces Europe),
the leadership of the Tactical Air Forces.*

*1990, with my deputy, Mike Kerby, and
PACAF's numbered air force commanders:
Tom McInerney (Eleventh Air Force),
J.B. Davis (Fifth Air Force),
Tom Baker (Seventh Air Force), and
Don Snyder (Thirteenth Air Force).*

Leaving Honolulu for Washington, November 1990.

Air Command as a major command and added another numbered air force, Eleventh, to PACAF.

In the process, I came to know and admire Ted Stevens. A former Air Corps pilot who had flown the "Hump" in World War II, Stevens was a John Wayne type, a great American. And Danny Inouye, an authentic American combat hero, was no slouch either.

We were lucky to have outstanding diplomatic representation in the Pacific. Mike Mansfield was in Japan during the first part of my tour. His successor, Mike Armacost, was a high-quality guy, very smart. In Malaysia, we had a first-rate diplomat in Paul Cleveland. Paul Wolfowitz, our guy in Indonesia, was among our most talented representatives. Off the charts bright, Wolfowitz was maybe a little unsure of himself, at least around senior military officers, but he was a nice man, married to a beautiful woman, a former Peace Corps volunteer in Indonesia.

Driving into Manila to meet with Minister of Defense (later, President) Fidel Ramos, I passed Smokey Mountain, an enormous trash heap that smoldered even when torrential rains lasted for weeks. Allegedly, this mountain of rubbish was the Philippines's fourth-largest city. Drawn to Manila by hopes of a better life, villagers squatted and mined the pitiful resource, a metaphor for the growing disaster of overpopulation and urban migration in poor countries.

I got in to see Ramos late in the evening, his duty day already extended. Supplicants crowded the office, and I didn't feel good about taking his time with a routine courtesy call. However, he was very gracious. This was my first chance to meet Ramos, a West Point graduate and classmate of Charlie Gabriel. The scene in his outer office reminded me how painful a politician's life must be.

In Korea and at Kunsan to observe a local readiness exercise, I noticed pilots were wearing empty holsters. Support officers did not even simulate being armed. I suppose this precaution sprang from some concern about safety. In any case, back in Honolulu, I ordered all combat units to issue loaded weapons whenever they exercised. As part of this Officer Arming Program, all officers, pilots and otherwise, received additional training with sidearms. This cost us some money for practice ammunition, but it was a good expense to incur. Too often, the Air Force seemed like a big, blue bureaucracy. We needed to start thinking like warriors.

Air chiefs from various parts of the globe met regularly with our chief of staff. An initiative of long standing brought together airmen of the Western Hemisphere. NATO air chiefs met regularly. However, we had no such gathering for the Pacific region, though several air forces in this region were important to us. I decided to start the Pacific Air Chiefs, issuing invitations to the heads of all air forces in the PACOM AOR, except those of North Korea, Vietnam, and New Zealand.[28] After much back and forth, the air chiefs of Australia (Ray Funnell), Brunei (Jocklin "Jock" bin Kongpaw), Japan (Tadayoshi Yonekawa), Malaysia (Mohamed "Matt" Ngah), Mongolia (Choijamtsyn Ulaanhu), the Philippines (Jose "Pepe" De Leon), and Singapore (Mike Teo) accepted. I subsidized travel of the Mongolian chief, a colonel who turned out to be not an airman, but a SAM shooter. This was his first contact with the West. He did not play golf, but neither did Ray Funnell, so the two of them rode a cart around and watched the rest of us hack away at the rough.

This first meeting of Pacific Air Chiefs featured briefings and social events in Honolulu, a quick trip to Washington to meet with Larry Welch, and, finally, visits to a few domestic Air Force bases. Naturally, meetings of this sort advanced the US agenda, but they

---

28 At the time, official relations with New Zealand were clouded by our (foolish) refusal to modify the "neither confirm nor deny" policy under which naval vessels visiting foreign ports-of-call could not declare whether they had nuclear materials aboard. A start on fixing this came in 1991, when President George Bush ordered tactical nuclear weapons removed from the US surface fleet.

also gave senior airmen a chance to get to know one another in a nonconfrontational setting—for some, the first such opportunity. Particularly for officers like Ulaanhu, the association was an important step in breaking out of isolation and, in Mongolia's case, domination by the former Soviet Union. Thus, in my judgment, organizing the Pacific Air Chiefs turned out to be a valuable contribution. The gathering became a tradition, occurring every other year and providing informal lines of communication among and between airmen of all Pacific nations.

Near the end of March 1989, the oil tanker Exxon Valdez poured 12 million gallons of crude into Prince William Sound in Alaska. Active Air Force units at Elmendorf and Eielson as well as the Alaska Air National Guard responded promptly to the worst oil spill in US history. Tom McInerney did a great job as on-scene commander. I had a ringside seat, since we were beginning to fold the Air Force in Alaska into PACAF.

From April through June 1989, an upheaval occurred in China. On 15 April, Hu Yaobang, a former party general secretary, died. Two days later, students took to the streets, an expression of respect for liberal ideas that had led to Hu's removal from office. By 16 May, a million people were protesting in Beijing. On 20 May, martial law was declared, and on 3 and 4 June regular troops cleared Tiananmen Square, killing an undetermined number. Zhao Ziyang, who had succeeded Hu, fell from power, apparently for not being hard enough on the protesters.

The Tiananmen Square massacre got mammoth press coverage in the West and upset the applecart in Washington and Honolulu. I thought we overreacted. Of course, our purposes do not require us to ignore what a repressive government does to its own citizens. We shouldn't look the other way on the issue of civil liberties or official human rights abuse. Nevertheless, as a commander with military responsibilities in the region, I was inclined to find ways to get along with the Chinese. They were large, they lived here, and they had nuclear ammunition. China was already a big player in the world economy, and its energetic, enterprising people would soon make it bigger, probably a lot bigger. The major recurring problem we had was the status of Taiwan, an issue President Nixon already conceded as part of the historic opening to China. The Chinese had never abandoned the objective of reunification (nor should we expect them to), but so far, they'd shown the patience to allow change to develop peacefully.

In thinking about our relations with China, I kept coming back to its future economic potential. My official duties took me just about everywhere in the region, and throughout Southeast Asia I ran into thriving overseas Chinese communities, Singapore the standout example. There, of course, as in Taiwan and Hong Kong, ethnic Chinese made up a majority of the population. Elsewhere, they were a minority and, if anything, too successful for their own good, sparking resentment that could take a murderous turn, as it had, for instance, in Indonesia. However, it seemed wherever they settled, the Chinese showed the commitment and skill needed for commercial success. There was no reason to think this point had been lost on the old men in Beijing. In interesting contrast to what Gorbachev was up to in Russia, the Chinese had made it clear they'd first do economic, then (maybe) political reform— *perestroika* before *glasnost*. This approach had its costs, keeping a lid on the student movement being one of them. Nevertheless, it was a much safer, sounder strategy, one that opened the prospect of great wealth and therefore great power, and we shouldn't fault them for choosing it.

Between August 1989 and the end of the year, Communist governments abdicated or ceased to exist in Poland, Czechoslovakia, Hungary, Romania, and Bulgaria, and did so without so much as a shot being fired, except in Romania. On 10 November 1989, the citizens of the German Democratic Republic pulled down the Berlin

Wall. Some formal structures—the Warsaw Pact, the Soviet Union itself—remained in place for a while, but the momentous events of the second half of 1989 marked the end of the Cold War.

On balance, we managed the long showdown with the Soviet Union rather badly, in my view. We dealt with nearly every international issue in the crude black-and-white of confrontation, hardly ever seeing shades of gray we could have turned to advantage. We did not forfeit our personal freedoms, though J. Edgar Hoover's shenanigans and the phase of McCarthyism show how close we came, and how little we cared. We fought major wars in Korea and Vietnam, each a different species of failure, and smaller, proxy wars in Africa and Latin America, the outcomes nearly always saddening. We spent more than $13 trillion, and though we didn't bankrupt ourselves, enormous opportunity costs were rolled into this staggering sum. Anyway, no like amount should have been needed against such disadvantaged opposition. At the policy level we were matched against a monochrome, heavy-footed bureaucracy handicapped by the obligation to market an unpopular design. Wherever tried, Communism was more or less synonymous with poverty. It's a good question how they managed to hold on as long as they did. Surely part of the answer is their system did deliver at least some of the things people everywhere want: a narrowed gap between the richest and poorest citizens, free universal schooling, the rudiments of a welfare state, including health care. These few accomplishments were real—in some of the cases, we have a ways to go ourselves—and without them, their own people surely would have overturned the system long before they finally did.

We assign ourselves, and to Ronald Reagan, especially, much glory, but the Chinese have nearly as good a claim to Cold War victory. The Sino-Soviet split, starting in earnest in 1960 and ending only after formal dissolution of the Soviet Union in 1991, was nearly coterminous with the Cold War and involved some actual, face-to-face fighting (along the Ussuri River in 1969). In effect, the Russians made Cold War on two fronts, a massive geopolitical handicap we didn't get around to leveraging until Nixon's trip in 1972. That some regard Nixon's altogether obvious move as proving his foreign-policy acumen is an indication of our tactical enfeeblement during this period.

We were lucky: the Soviets more than matched our mistakes. Their last big one, the hapless intervention in Afghanistan, led to an unraveling, pushed along with China's (again) mostly unacknowledged help. In the end, the Cold War wasn't so much our win as Russia's loss. We should be thankful but humble. It was a close-run thing, and, anyway, there's little to celebrate in a success compounded of fewer failures.

We can say—and it is no trivial claim—that the sides built tens of thousands of nuclear weapons, kept many of them on high alert for decades, and did not blow up the world. Moreover, the nuclear embrace made every war dangerous for everybody, a condition that at the margins produced more measured and moderate behavior, fewer cases of thoughtless escalation, less conflict growing out of miscalculation. Everyone understood that, at the high end of the spectrum, the best use of force was not to use it at all.

But now we entered a phase in which we could no longer rely on even this slender dividend. Going forward, armed conflict would be more assessable. With constraining influences less evident, we could anticipate a renaissance of war. Rather than a threat-free world, we were entering one less ordered, more shaped by forces we did not yet understand, perhaps even more dangerous.

Now, too, the collapse of Soviet central institutions left us alone at the top of the heap, the sole entity possessing in full measure all the instruments of national power—economic, diplomatic, political, and, of course, military. In many ways, and probably only temporarily, we were the only country that mattered, an unpredicted result. While the condition lasted, we would find ourselves propelled into action against secondary but nevertheless powerful forces that until now had remained frozen in place by the Cold War. For a while, at least, national safety would depend on whether we gave power to leaders wise enough to manage a world completely unlike the one in which we had found ourselves for two generations. On this score, our track record in my lifetime did not make me hopeful.

Corazon Aquino came to power in Manila atop a wave of expectation that she could undo many of the wrongs piled up by Marcos. When this proved hard to do, Filipino disillusionment culminated in a coup attempt led by military dissidents, including some elements of the Philippine Air Force. Aquino asked for our help. Along with other measures, President Bush approved using fighter aircraft stationed at Clark to buzz rebel planes, an action that soon caused the coup to collapse.

In the spring of 1990, Secretary of the Air Force Don Rice and his wife, Susan, visited the headquarters. Ellie and I hosted the Rices for a couple of days, part of an interview process to select a new chief of staff. I was told the other officer in the hunt was my old friend Mike Dugan, in command of our forces in Europe.

In thinking about my prospects of becoming chief, I saw both pluses and minuses. On the plus side, I'd done a reasonably good job as commander of successively larger chunks of Air Force business. At every level, I'd quickly established goals, made them few and easily understood, and pushed them hard. I'd made clear my belief in the primacy of human factors in combat: organization, training, discipline, and good tactics riding on top of—and, in a crunch, being more important than—advanced hardware. I'd pressed the notion of a warrior ethic, emphasizing toughness and physical fitness. This approach had put PACAF (and previously, Twelfth Air Force and before that the 20th Wing) in the best fighting condition ever.

I'd built PACAF, adding Guam's Andersen AFB and Alaska's Eleventh Air Force. I'd shown myself to be a cost-conscious, efficient administrator. A "war on paperwork" had reduced the number of PACAF regulations, manuals, policy letters, and so forth, by about half. Concerned with overhead, I'd proposed a one-third cut in my own staff and had frozen civilian hiring in October 1989, well before the OSD had done the same thing. I'd acted immediately and effectively to recover savings when we closed or phased down PACAF installations.

On the "jointness" front, I'd been an effective advocate of Air Force positions while at the same time understanding where the Air Force fit in the context of a joint effort. My relationship with successive theater CINCs, Fred Woerner, Ron Hays, and Hunt Hardisty, had been a sort of "love-in." I'd gotten along well with the leadership of other services, especially David Jeremiah, former fleet commander in the Pacific, who had moved on to be Colin Powell's deputy as vice-chairman of the JCS. I'd established myself as a booster of the Total Force, with a record of support for the Air National Guard and Air Force Reserve. I'd given a big shot in the arm to air-force-to-air-force relationships in the Pacific, establishing personal friendships with the region's principal air chiefs.

I could claim to be a sort of junior-grade defense intellectual, a member of the Council on Foreign Relations and of London's International Institute for Strategic Studies. I'd published journal articles. Right or wrong, I did not believe there was anybody in any service who had thought harder or knew more about how to fight an air war in a theater of operations.

On the other hand, I was not a hardware guy, knowing little (and perhaps not caring as much as I should) about equipment procurement, a huge issue for the chief of staff. I had affection for and deep pride in the people who worked for me, but nobody would describe me as a warm and cuddly personality. Finally, and perhaps decisively, I was something of a maverick. In his brilliant Vietnam classic *To What End*, Ward Just observes:

> Initiative can propel a man from captain to major, and sometimes from major to lieutenant colonel. But at that point caution commends itself. In the American military services, expressions of conventional wisdom are raised to the level of an art form.

With apologies to Mr. Just, conventional wisdom wasn't my style. Certainly, by comparison with Mike Dugan, I would be seen as something of a wild card.

One doesn't really "run" for senior military posts—or perhaps better said, one does so carefully, feigned indifference being part of the job specification. So I did the best I could with Dr. and Mrs. Rice, without (I hoped) giving the impression that becoming chief much interested me. Mike Dugan's pluses were as strong as mine, and maybe he had fewer minuses. In any event, it soon became clear I'd come in second. In July, Mike was sworn in as the Air Force's 13th chief of staff.

On 2 August 1990, beginning at 2:00 a.m. local time, troops of the Iraqi Republican Guard crossed the border into Kuwait. Kuwaiti armed forces managed to resist in a few isolated pockets but could not prevent Iraqi armored units from reaching their objectives, and the entire country was overrun quickly. The emir of Kuwait and large numbers of his countrymen fled to Saudi Arabia. Later that day, the UN Security Council met in emergency session and passed a resolution condemning the invasion and calling for immediate withdrawal of Iraqi forces.

Secretary of Defense Dick Cheney; Gen. Norman Schwarzkopf, commander of Central Command (CENTCOM), the joint head-quarters responsible for the region; and Lt. Gen. Chuck Horner, head of CENTCOM's Air Force component, flew to Saudi Arabia for discussions. Cheney and Schwarzkopf returned to Washington, but Horner stayed, in command of CENTCOM Forward. When King Fahd invited foreign governments to send troops to Saudi Arabia to head off Iraqi attack, President Bush immediately ordered the large-scale movement of military forces into the region.

At the time of Iraq's invasion, the Navy's Middle East Group consisted of the command ship *La Salle* and a small force of sup-porting cruisers, destroyers, and frigates on exercise in the Persian Gulf. The carrier *Independence* and its battle group steamed just outside the area, in the Gulf of Oman. The nearest Air Force unit was at Incirlik Air Base, in southern Turkey, but this rotational training base had no aircraft permanently assigned. The nearest Army units were on the continent of Europe.

By 8 August two squadrons of F-15s from Langley AFB arrived at Dhahran, having flown nonstop, the longest operational fighter deployment in history. The Ready Brigade of 2,300 paratroopers from the 82nd Airborne Division came in with the F-15s. The Eisenhower battle group moved out of the Mediterranean, cleared the Suez Canal and entered the Red Sea, and a force of B-52s commenced deployment to the island of Diego Garcia in the Indian Ocean. On 10 August, the Pentagon announced a name for the operation: Desert Shield.

Through mid- and late-August, formations from every service continued to file in. By 20 August, Horner had on hand squadrons flying the A-10, C-130, AWACS, F-4G, F-15, F-15E, F-16, KC-135, and KC-10 aircraft. Elements of the 101st Airborne and 24th Mechanized Infantry Divisions were added to the 82nd. *USS Kennedy*, the last conventionally powered aircraft carrier built for the Navy, left Norfolk with its battle group on 15 August and moved to join the *Independence*, though neither carrier entered the Gulf until the *Independence* did so on 4 October. In a glare of publicity, 22 F-117 stealth aircraft arrived in-theater on 21 August. Horner now assessed he had sufficient strength to defend Saudi Arabia against an Iraqi invasion.

In my view, this standing-start, 8,000-mile transfer of forces and equipment to the Gulf, accomplished within 18 days of the invasion of Kuwait, is the most impressive military maneuver in history. C-141s and C-5s from Military Airlift Command and chartered civilian cargo aircraft moved virtually all the people and high-priority equipment. (Sealift brought in bulk fuel and ammo.) Hundreds of Strategic Air Command KC-10 and KC-135 tankers provided aerial refueling for lift and combat aircraft. We built a virtual aluminum bridge over the North Atlantic.

To put what we did in context, the common measure of airlift capacity is millions of ton-miles (MTM) per day. In World War II, the famous Flying Tigers managed to lift less than one MTM per day over the Hump into China. During the Berlin airlift, we about doubled the Hump effort, flying 1.7 MTM per day into the city. For Desert Shield, we increased the Berlin effort by an order of magnitude, delivering 17 MTM per day. We brought in more than 482,000 passengers and 513,000 tons of air cargo, the equivalent of moving Oklahoma City—its citizens, their possessions, vehicles, furniture, everything—to the other side of the planet, then feeding and sustaining them for the duration. Nobody else in the world could have done this. This aspect of American power—our air mobility—makes us unique, gives us a priceless capability to influence events in any part of the globe.

On 29 August, a C-5 carrying cargo bound for Saudi Arabia crashed on takeoff from Ramstein Air Base, Germany, killing 13 of 17 souls on board. This was the first aircraft loss and these the first casualties of the Gulf War.

Although the principal air route to the Gulf stretched across the North Atlantic, some movement through the Pacific occurred, especially in connection with the B-52 deployment to Diego Garcia. Much of the support moved through Andersen AFB, now belonging to PACAF. I made sure we turned out in force to help SAC's effort. In addition, some PACAF F-4s from the Philippines deployed to the Gulf. We did what we could, but PACAF was well away from the center of the action.

On 31 August, the Pentagon announced my nomination for reassignment as commander of Tactical Air Command, replacing Bob Russ, slated to retire 1 February 1991. Lt. Gen. Jimmie Adams, the serving DCS for plans and operations, would take over PACAF. I was delighted at the prospect of going to this great job. However, as incumbent Chief of Staff Mike Dugan and Secretary Rice worked their way through a revised game plan for senior officers,

they apparently had second thoughts. Mike called to say I'd be stay-ing in Honolulu, and Adams would go to command TAC instead. This did not sit well with me, not least because my nomination had already been made public. I began to spend more time thinking about retirement from active duty.

In mid-September, Mike Dugan went to the Gulf to check on prog-ress, taking along several general officers, plus Rick Atkinson of the *Washington Post*, John Morocco of *Aviation Week*, and John Broder of the *Los Angeles Times*. His inspection tour completed and back on the airplane headed home, Dugan held an impromptu press conference. He made a number of predictions about the oncoming engagement, seeming to promote the Air Force's role, to the disad-vantage of the other services. Some of the formulations were color-ful—the sort of thing that eats up headlines. (One widely reported quotation had Mike saying, "The best way to hurt Saddam is to target his family, his personal guard, and his mistress.") Dugan's remarks were printed in full in Sunday editions. JCS Chairman Colin Powell was livid. So was Secretary of Defense Dick Cheney, who invited Dugan downstairs first thing Monday morning.

Early in his tenure, Cheney had shown a readiness to take peo-ple to the woodshed, publicly wire-brushing Larry Welch for some off-the-record discussions with congressmen about the future deployment of land-based ballistic missiles, just then a hot topic. In my view, Welch had been innocent in the matter, a bum rap caus-ing much puzzlement inside the Air Force. Nonetheless, Cheney was just possibly waiting for somebody else to test him. Dugan had done so with a vengeance.

On Monday morning, 17 September 1990, Dugan called me to say he'd been fired. In Honolulu, six hours behind Washington, he woke me from a sound sleep. He said Mike Loh, the vice chief, would take over as "acting" but guessed I'd hear something shortly. Indeed, at 2:30 p.m. East Coast time the same day, Secretary Cheney announced his intention to nominate me as the new Air

Force chief of staff. Secretary of the Air Force Donald Rice released a statement at 4:00 p.m.:

> I regret the circumstances that made it necessary for Secretary of Defense Dick Cheney to take this action. General Dugan is a superb officer. His leadership and innovation will be missed by every man and woman in the Air Force.
>
> I'm pleased that Secretary Cheney has accepted my recommendation of Gen. Merrill A. McPeak to succeed General Dugan as chief of staff.

At Rice's direction, I flew to Washington a week later, on Monday, 24 September, to meet with him and others. He advised me to keep a low profile. Nothing damages prospects of Senate confirmation so much as acting as though it's assured. I was to stay completely away from the chief's office—fly in from time to time but, for the most part, stay in Hawaii and tend to business. OK by me.

It was easy to follow Rice's advice, at least at first. I flew back to Hawaii on 26 September, having shown my face in our nation's capital for all of one day. I returned to Washington on Monday, 1 October, for meetings on Capitol Hill, and afterward went right back to the islands. I logged what turned out to be my last F-15 sortie with the Hawaii Air National Guard on 5 October.

After that it got harder to stay away from the Pentagon. The buildup in the Gulf continued, and I wanted to be in the loop. In addition, I needed to do some schmoozing in the run-up to Senate confirmation. I flew back to Washington on 8 October, spent two weeks there, returned to Hickam to pack furniture on the 20th, and went back to Washington on the 23rd. The Senate confirmed my nomination as chief of staff on 27 October 1990. I returned to Hawaii for a round of farewells, then came back to Washington and was sworn in as the Air Force's 14th chief of staff on Wednesday morning, 7 November 1990.

Logbook: PACAF, 1988–90

F-15A	92.8
F-15B	11.2
F-15C	15.1
F-15D	7.3
Total F-15	126.4

Appendix: Notices to Airmen

Principles of War: Since Sun Tzu's *Art of War*, strategists have offered lists of principles which, if followed, are reckoned to ensure victory. Usually, the lists are short, though with typical thoroughness Napoleon laid down 115 items he called maxims. There is much harmony in the various lists, but each is just different enough that generals cannot build a simple checklist for battlefield use. That, and the unhappy fact that the principles are often at cross-purposes (contrast, for instance, the need to achieve both "mass" and "surprise") help explain why war remains what Sun Tzu called an art.

History shows that generals do not always understand the principles of war, hard to explain because they are so easily grasped. And if we know anything about war, it is that these principles work, for every kind of warfare. So good generals study and try to implement them. A sign of greatness in a general is the willingness to imagine how some principle of war might be violated in order to make one or more of the others decisive. Here, for what it's worth, is my list:

Objective: Aim at a clearly defined target.

Precision: Hit what you aim at.

Unity of Command: Make one person responsible.

Simplicity: Prepare uncomplicated plans and issue clear orders.

Initiative: Be active, even (or especially) on the defensive.

Flexibility: Adapt to changing circumstances.

Maneuver: Move to keep the enemy off balance.

Speed: Act quickly, before he can adjust.

Surprise: Attack unprepared defenses.

Because surprise is so important, I make separate entries for maneuver, speed, and surprise, though a bond of intimacy is obvious. Surprise, if you can achieve it, will come close to settling the matter.

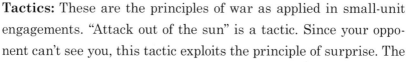

Tactics: These are the principles of war as applied in small-unit engagements. "Attack out of the sun" is a tactic. Since your opponent can't see you, this tactic exploits the principle of surprise. The ambush is another well-understood tactic, effective for the same reason.

If principles of war are for generals, then tactics are the stock in trade of captains. Here, introspection is not a requirement. We judge captains by their ability to execute.

Doctrine: The principles of war and the tactics used at the sharp end are clear and well-enough defined. Doctrine, on the other hand, is a sort of moving fog bank. Sun Tzu calls doctrine one of the five "fundamental factors" in war, though in his translation Griffith explains that the character used, *fa*, has the primary meaning of "law," or "method." Griffith has Sun Tzu describe doctrine as "organization, control, assignment of appropriate ranks to officers, regulation of supply routes, and the provision of principal items used by the army." Compare this suspect description with Sun Tzu's usually straightforward advice, like: "Fight downhill," or "Treat captives well."

The problem is not with Sun Tzu, but with the term itself. Here is a modern definition, sponsored by the US Department of Defense and picked up in an edition of NATO's Glossary of Terms and Definitions: "Fundamental principles by which military forces guide their actions in support of objectives. It is authoritative but requires judgment in application." This definition makes one wonder why and how doctrine is different from the principles of war, or even tactics. The same bicycle pump has been at work on a definition plucked at random from the Internet: "The concise expression of how military forces contribute to campaigns, major operations, battles, and engagements." We await that "conciseness" with impatience, hoping it starts with agreement about what the word means. It's not clear, for instance, that the two definitions cited in this paragraph describe the same thing.

Notwithstanding the uncertainty about what it is, precisely, each of the US services cranks out doctrine. Since much service doctrine is at odds with that of other services, it cannot all be correct.

In recent years, the chairman of the Joint Chiefs of Staff has required the production of joint doctrine. The Army's view of the battlefield is the more faithfully represented in the resulting publications, reflecting an expertise assiduously developed over the years. It might have been better simply to have adopted Army doctrine outright. Though it is in my view wrong in some respects, Army doctrine has a sort of internal consistency. On the other hand, committee work reaches near perfection in the joint doctrine documents produced so far, a family of little Frankensteins stitched together using doctrinal cadavers from the individual services. To the extent this body of work is read at all, it can be and is interpreted differently by each service, with the result that it is anything but helpful in preparing forces to fight as part of a joint team.

Air Doctrine: Airmen should think about doctrine, and I have, without much to show for the effort. No one should give up just because I've been unsuccessful; others may be able to write clear sentences that add substance to our understanding of how to apply airpower. The best I can do is a modest description of how airpower fits into our theoretical understanding of armed conflict more generally considered. That is, what appears below is not doctrine so much as a set of facts that should be accounted for when formulating doctrine. (And good luck with that.)

Traditional military thought has focused on defeating an opponent in close battle through a combination of direct attrition or (better, in my opinion) maneuver, leading to the threat of direct attrition. But maneuver at the earth's surface is mightily influenced by constraints of geography and time. On land (and in large measure also at sea), battle formations, plans, and operations are determined first by geographic features like rivers, mountains, islands, and so forth, and second by the time it takes to move people and equipment slowed by the drag of surface contact. Freed of terrestrial constraints, air forces have always been maneuver forces *par excellence*, moving much faster and over vastly extended distances. Moreover, they pose an attrition threat wherever they appear.

Air forces can accomplish the direct attrition of front line forces and in some cases this will be their best use. But more often, airmen should maneuver over and past the front line to attack important targets in the rear, in this way contributing a lot more to the success of other theater war-fighting components. Thus, dividing the air effort as we so often have, based on geography, the measured pace of ground maneuver, or a local commander's direct attrition objective, automatically results in wasteful, less effective use of airpower.

All this seemed clear to early airmen, who should have been content with the sufficient claim that airpower, properly used, would have a decisive influence on the outcome of battle at the earth's surface. But they made the more impassioned argument that relatively bloodless victory was possible through airpower alone. This view was discredited during the Second World War, when the mighty Eighth Air Force was able to achieve average miss distances no better than about a kilometer, in what was called precision daylight bombing. With this sort of "precision" you have to send a whole lot of bombers against things like ball bearing factories, which is why your likelihood of being killed before completing the required 30 missions was 71 percent. In the Second World War, more US servicemen died in the Air Corps than in the Marine Corps. So much for easy victory.

But we learned a lot about this new instrument of war, in Europe and the Pacific, in Korea and Vietnam. By the early 1990s, we'd invented the technology—guided munitions—that made for purposeful direct attrition. A changed organizational culture was even more important: we were led, finally, by officers who had spent their entire professional lives in a blue uniform, thinking about and practicing the uses of airpower. So, we have begun to see the early promise of airpower realized, at least for Type A War.

Centralized Control, Decentralized Execution: This is a much misunderstood, but nevertheless basic tenent for employing airpower.

The air battle should be organized according to the ideas of an airman given responsibility for its concept and structure, then fought by airmen leading forces at the point of attack. All have welcomed the second part of this formulation because it gives subordinate commanders plenty of scope and the flexibility to respond rapidly to changing circumstances. Centralized control has not been popular, for the most part honored in the breach even within the Air Force. Though the need to integrate forces and capabilities working together would seem obvious, the Air Force has often put only "tactical" units under unambiguous theater command. Strategic Air Command went to great lengths to retain control of bombers and tankers, wherever and for whatever purpose they were assigned. Military Airlift Command sought to do the same thing, often retaining command even of smaller, short-range transports based and used exclusively in-theater. This approach impeded unity of Air Force operations, a big problem in both Korea and Vietnam, to say nothing of our integration with everybody else flying in a theater of operations.

If the Air Force itself has been reluctant to consolidate air capabilities and put them at the disposal of a single commander, the other services have stonewalled, or tried to. Even for so self-evident a case as nuclear attack into the old Soviet Union, the Navy had to be dragged kicking and screaming into the Joint Strategic Target

Planning Staff (JSTPS), which for many years produced nuclear strike plans that integrated manned bombers, aerial tankers, land-based ICBMs, submarine-based SLBMs, and associated reconnaissance assets. But in many ways, large-scale nuclear attack is a relatively uncomplicated problem. By contrast, integrating perhaps thousands of Air Force, Navy, Marine Corps, Special Operations, Army, and Allied aircraft so that the various categories of conventional aerial attack are aimed at the right targets, at the right time, with the right refueling, reconnaissance, electronic warfare, and other support, and doing so without fratricide in what may be a rather small operating area, and doing it every day for weeks, or months, or years—that's hard. That's what requires centralized control.

———◆———

Joint Forces Air Component Commander (JFACC): It should be obvious that only integrated air operations are safe, reasonably affordable, and effective when the going gets tough. (Against second-rate opposition, you can be as badly organized as you like and still win, though of course you'll pay an unnecessarily high price in men and money.) However, US forces are saddled with a joint command and control structure that has no formal air component. Instead, in joint operations, each of the service components, the Army, Navy, Marine Corps, Air Force, and Special Operations Force, commands and, to a very considerable degree, controls its own air arm.

The battlefield integration issue is on its way to an imperfect solution as a consequence of Goldwater-Nichols reforms that put much increased authority in the hands of joint commanders. Joint commanders are very likely to decide that at least the assigned air combat assets with any reach—that is, all combat aircraft not tied absolutely to the Close Air Support role—will be centrally tasked at theater level. To do the tasking, joint commanders will likely establish what is for the moment called a Joint Force Air Component Commander, or JFACC. (As noted above, there isn't any joint "air component," so it's a nice question just what the Joint Force Air Component Commander commands.)

In theory, the joint commander can choose a JFACC from any service. There will be qualified airmen in the aviation branches of each of the service components, and in the air element of the assigned Special Operations Force. But the unified command's Air Force Component is unambiguously the joint commander's own air arm and, except for special cases, no one else is likely to be designated JFACC. (As this is written, the aviation arms of the other services are in any case not organized or equipped to do theater-wide tasking of joint and/or combined air campaigns.)

If we're going to create an "air component" and put it under centralized command in combat, why not organize this way in peacetime? Good question, one that shows clearly why the other services have been unenthusiastic about the JFACC concept. They can be expected to fight what they regard as a hostile takeover of their air arms; the JFACC is in for lengthy and tendentious negotiation, with the joint commander acting as referee. This is no way to run a railroad, but it's what we're stuck with as a consequence of our failure to consolidate combat aviation when establishing a separate Air Force in 1947.

Argument Against Integration: The best argument other services have against industrial-strength integration of their air combat arms with those of the Air Force is this: while existing theater command and control structures can produce a sort of clumsy centralized control (under a JFACC), these same structures are simply incompatible with decentralized execution. They are correct. This is a good argument but (hopefully) only for the moment.

The problem is the time it takes to plan tomorrow's air operations. Forces that will participate are spread out all over the theater, at air bases and aboard ships dealing with their own constraints arising from local resource availability. At headquarters, targets have to be selected; munitions' loads specified; refueling tracks picked; electronic warfare, reconnaissance, and rescue forces positioned; radio frequencies selected. All this has to be phased and timed, typically for a 24-hour period. Then an order describing this complex, time-phased operation must be encrypted and dispatched to units early, so they can do their own planning, load weapons, brief crews, check weather, and so forth. The complexity of the planning task, the communications bandwidth required, and the difficulty of making modifications on the fly leads to rigidity in execution, robbing airpower of much of its flexibility, the feature that constitutes its crown jewel.

Better combat aircraft will need less help. For instance, stealth reduces the requirement for electronic warfare support. Modern on-board video systems give better feedback on results, obviating the need for post-strike reconnaissance. The air refueling requirement seems unlikely to go away soon; even so, we can visualize a tasking system that features much reduced complexity and allows for much more free play at the point of contact, all of which will undermine the logic supporting decentralized command of air operations.

Mission-Type Orders (*Auftragstaktik*): Notwithstanding the Hollywood version, our troops rarely outperformed the Germans in the Second World War. Many have argued (and I'm convinced) that a major reason for Germany's excellence in small-unit operations was their practice of decentralized decision making.

Mission-type orders communicate the commander's overall intent and direct that subordinates achieve desired operational outcomes in support of that intent. The elements of commander guidance will always include *why*, may or may not include *who*, *what*, and *when*, and should never include *how*.

This all seems pretty straightforward, the armed services of many countries giving much lip service to similar ideas. But the Germans were serious. *Auftragstaktik* was a sort of attitude, hard to explain because it so often involved what was *not* done.

Subordinates had the freedom even to disobey orders, if that was necessary to accomplish the objective.

Reliance on mission-type orders is to my way of thinking the only command technique that has much chance of success in what I elsewhere call Type B war. But we can rightly be skeptical about its implementation because, at a minimum, it involves taking career risk, a leadership style not normally associated with large bureaucracies.

Airborne Command and Control: The future central nervous system of battle puts the commander above the battlefield using sensors for situation awareness and communications links with combat forces in the air and on the surface.

Douglas Bader did something like this in aerial engagements during the World War II air defense of the British Isles. Flying to a vantage point, Bader sized up the air situation and gave direction to friendly fighters as the fight unfolded. In Southeast Asia, airborne command and control aircraft like "Hillsboro" tried to do the same sort of thing with respect to out-country interdiction. Without much in the way of on-board sensors, they could not respond quickly to changing circumstances and ended up playing a scorekeeping role. Nonetheless, even a rudimentary system like Hillsboro was so important that, had the North put up anything like it, we would have paid the price to knock it down.

Since stationary targets—buildings, bridges, airfields—can be reduced at will, the core issue is controlling attack of mobile targets in real time. To work this problem, much of the command and control apparatus—and the most effective part—has been moved into the air. Since Vietnam, the Air Force has fielded the Airborne Warning and Control System (AWACS) to handle air targets, and the Joint Surveillance and Targeting System (JSTARS) to do the much same thing for movers.

These airborne systems are good examples of the idea of

"centralized control, decentralized execution." Someone in the control aircraft, with access to the big picture, commits forces. Someone close to the target applies munitions. But because AWACS and JSTARS are airplanes (and *only* because of this), there has been heated debate about how this new technology should be used. Reflecting their ground-centric thinking, European military professionals could not agree that AWACS should have a control function. They named their version of the airplane AEW—Airborne Early Warning, stripping out the "C." They wanted the airplane to monitor and report the air situation to someone on the ground, who would exercise control. The US Army had similar reservations regarding JSTARS, directing that surface targets be tracked and the information reported to a ground commander who retained decision authority. As can be seen, the debate is really about who's in charge of selecting targets.

As we evolve to airborne systems that incorporate ever more powerful sensor suites and communications links, the debate will become more acrimonious, with surface-based commanders seeing themselves losing authority. Nevertheless, the flow of technology is rapid and inexorable. Airborne command and control is already a dominating factor, the brains of modern conflict, and will become more so. Without regard for country or service affiliation, the commander who wants to prevail will have to get in an airplane.

Put tankers and combat aircraft on airborne and ground alert, with a variety of munitions loads. Task these aircraft to report directly to an airborne commander for direction, targeting, and control. We already have decades of experience with aircraft like the AWACS and JSTARS, specialized for decentralized execution of the air and surface battle. We know it works.

The main idea is simplicity itself: accelerate *Auftragstaktik* to jet speeds.

Index

Page locators in *italics* indicate photographs.

Carter, Jimmy, 71, 89, 131, 207

Castro, Fidel, 181

Central America, 179–84

Central Command (CENTCOM), 225

Central Region Air Operations Center
(CRAOC), 90

Chain, Jack, 211

Charles, Prince of Wales, 113

Cheney, Dick, 19, 180*n*20, 225, 228–29

Cherry, Fred, 37

chief of staff duties, Ramstein, 129–30

Chile, 181

China: foreign military sales, 168–70;
foreign relations, 219–20

Christie, Julie, 123, 124

Churchill, John, 112–13

Churchill, Winston, 113, 158

Cimino, Michael, 79

Clarence (pet cat), 8

classified material, excess, 203–4

Cleveland, Paul, 217

Clinton, Bill, 136

close air support (CAS), 157

Cold War, 22–23, 99–100, 102, 122, 181,
191, 221–23

collateral investigations, 48–50

Colonel Timon, Zaragoza, 79, 80–81, 82

combat support group commander
duties, 67

command and control: airborne
command and control, 239–40; the
Bunker, 86–88, 90–92, 94–98

command duties, Pacific Air Forces, 197,
202–4, 210–12, 217

command post, 20th Wing, 103–4, 112,
117

command priorities, 20th Wing, 110–12

commander in chief of Pacific Air Forces
(CINCPACAF), 191–92, 210, *213*

commander in chief of Pacific Command
(CINCPAC), 192, 205

Communism and the Cold War, 221–23

complaints resolution, Zaragoza, 77

Concepts Division, equipment
acquisition, 148

Cope Thunder training program, 199

Coppola, Francis Ford, 80

Cost of Living Council, 19

Cotswolds, 101

Council on Foreign Relations: *Foreign
Affairs* article, 56, 61; Military
Fellow duties, 53–54

counterterrorism, 210

Cox, Archibald, 40

Creech, Wilbur L. "Bill," 32, 74, 138–40,
145–46, 149, 152–54, 161–63, *194*

Crow, Fred, 37

Crowe, Bill, 135–36

Cuba, 181

D

Davis, Bennie, 153

Davis, J. B., 197–98, *215*

Davis, Jefferson, 150

Dayan, Moshe, 25, 33–34

De Leon, Jose "Pepe," 218

Deacon, Gladys, 113

Delta Force, Special Operations Force
(SOF), 206–8

Department of Defense (DOD), 21–22

deputy for maintenance (DM) duties,
66–67

deputy for operations (DO) duties, 65,
67, 68

deputy for resource management (RM)
duties, 66–67

deputy for plans duties, 146–49

Desert Shield, 147, 226–27

Desert Storm, 146

Dewey, Arthur "Gene," 54

Dixon, Bob, 32, 47, 139

doctrine: dogma vs. doctrine, 164;
principles of war, 138, 155, 232–35;
TAC-TRADOC doctrine dialogue,
154–62, 163–64

Domesday Book, 63

Dominican Republic, 181

Doolittle, Jimmy, 175

Dougherty, Russ, 9

Douglas, William O., 28–29

Douhet, Giulio, 129, 157

Dozier, James, 131

driver training, antiterrorist, 134

Dugan, Michael J., 126, 139–40, 174,
215, 223, 225, 227–29

Dulles, Allen, 181

Dulles, John Foster, 181

Dutton, Dick, 37

E

Eagle Claw hostage rescue attempt, 207

Eberhart, Ralph E. "Ed," 129–30, 130*n*8

Ebro Valley, 75, 78

Eddins, Neil, 130

Ehrlichman, John, 29

Eisenhower, Dwight D., 22, 176*n*18

ejection seats: F-4 aircraft, 46; F-16
aircraft, 177; F-111 aircraft, 107